HM Forces Summary Justice System

- A Dissertation -

September 2017

I0415364

Published, edited and submitted by
Edd King and the Author D Cochrane May 2019

Copyright © David Cochrane 2017

David Cochrane MSc; MRes; Cert Ed.

for

Dissertation submitted as partial requirement for the award

of

Master's in Research

in

Humanities and Social Sciences

University of Portsmouth

We are obliged to the Office of the Judge Advocate General for its assistance in this research and in particular to HHJ Jeff Blackett, JAG., to and Miles Rowley, Deputy Director Military Court Service, Upavon, Wiltshire.

CONTENTS

Abstract

Supplementary Information:

ABSTRACT

We are fortunate that in this country we do not have to look beyond our shores for a form of summary justice that is fair to all who might at some time or other engage with the criminal justice system. However, and whether it be for historical reasons or for the convenience of the relevant authorities, there is a substantial number of people subject to a form of summary justice not wholly identifiable with that of the civil courts. Theirs is an inquisitorial process applied by unqualified personnel who are not bound by the rules of evidence, where the accused are not permitted legal representation, and there are *inter alia* serious questions to its independence and impartiality.

Bad enough this might be to whomsoever it applies, but the individuals referred to here are the 150,000 or so members of the UK Armed Forces, and there is no group of people more deserving of fairer treatment by their own officers, the Ministry of Defence and HM Government than they, and which should be at least as fair as that which applies to the civilian population.

This little booklet [based on the dissertation] will set out *in extenso* the service justice system and compare it to the procedures applied in the civilian courts and which in operation ensure that nobody is convicted of any offence without a fair hearing and where there is any doubt as to his guilt. This is facilitated because the machinery of justice in England and Wales is operated, managed and overseen by legal professionals; the way evidence is presented, its admissibility or otherwise, the capacity of the accused, the degree of credibility given to each witness and to every document, the definition of the offence, and any harm occasioned thereby and the suitability of any order or sentence made after a finding of guilt, all has a part to play in the process. Magistrates' and Judges' respective roles in the administration of justice are many, but it is predominantly to ensure that the process is fairly conducted.

In HM Forces however, officers managing the summary process deal equally with criminal and disciplinary matters, and the decisions taken at those hearings can impact adversely on a serviceman even after he has returned to civilian life, maybe many years later, as summary convictions, be it for criminal or disciplinary offences, can be recorded on the Police National Computer.

This, after a process over which hangs a question as to its independence and impartiality and its fairness, surely demands close scrutiny and if appropriate, change to certain of its procedures and, if necessary, the personnel involved.

The current system has been the *status quo* for many years, maybe for historical reasons, even though the service justice system is supposedly subject to a 5-yearly review; the last review was in 2016 where no significant changes were made, but it is hoped that the Board will use the 2021 review to effect a long overdue *root and branch* overhaul engendered by, amongst other things, the involvement of the European Convention of Human Rights, now, and lately, used to challenge decisions made in the higher, Courts Martial proceedings and the criticisms of which impact equally on the summary processes.

Hence the recommendations which follow; the aim is to give the servicemen not only a fair hearing, but to treat them in a way which is right bearing in mind their role in the defence of the UK and the sometimes harsh conditions they endure which at the very least suggests that they should be treated at least as fairly as the civilian population.

1. INTRODUCTION.

This dissertation will examine the hypothesis that the Summary Justice process as applied in Her Majesty's Armed Forces does not offer the same safeguards defendants would have in civilian courts and is therefore inherently unfair to the accused.

It is understandable that HM Forces have a need to deal with the soldiers, sailors and airmen of all ranks who commit criminal offences, and where they are not referred to the civil Magistrates' or Crown courts, but what is difficult to understand is why these proceedings are so far removed from the process as applied in the civilian courts, as to be almost unrecognisable and as a result does not offer, or apparently offer, a fair system of justice but yet can apply all or most of the sanctions which can be 'handed down' by the civilian courts.

Rant [2009] points out that discipline is an essential element of command, so as regards the handling of disciplinary offences, it is advantageous for the for the Services to have the facility to pursue those offences within their own units and with minimum delay but it must be done in a way which is beyond criticism and is fair to the accused. However, the process has, as with criminal hearings, to be applied fairly and impartially.

It may well be that in the past there was an operational need to deal with transgressors 'in the field' and where there was no practical alternative to ensure that justice was swift and effective in maintaining discipline. However, today this is rarely if ever necessary especially in view of the fact that Her Majesty's Government maintains at great expense a comprehensive and professionally-staffed organisation concerned purely with the administration of justice in all three of the UK Armed Forces.

The foregoing raises a number of questions, and all will be addressed comprehensively. The questions are as follows:

1. Why does the Ministry of Defence [MOD] operate a system of summary justice based on procedures which are not recognised by UK civilian courts?

This encompasses the main element of the hypothesis, viz., when compared with civilian summary courts, the military criminal-cases process does not reflect the safeguards an accused would have in the Magistrates' courts. The Service summary hearings are not regarded as a 'court' so the rules of evidence do not apply and nor is the accused afforded legal representation when in front of his Commanding Officer. [henceforth the male gender will include the female gender]. One has to ask whether this is a 'fiction' for the convenience for the Service at the expense of giving the accused a fair hearing, or whether there are always overriding operational reasons why normal court etiquette is not followed.

2. Why does the same process apply equally in criminal cases and to non-criminal, e.g., disciplinary matters?

No civilian court empowered to hear criminal cases will ever deal with non-criminal, employment and disciplinary matters but within HM Forces such matters are dealt with by the same tribunal, and certain non-criminal 'convictions' on disciplinary offences can be registered on the police national computer [PNC] but this does not apply to the outcome of any civilian employment / disciplinary cases. In addition, certain disciplinary matters can be dealt with by non-commissioned personnel, of rank from corporal or equivalent, but subject to review 'at a higher level than it was initiated'. For the person who feels himself to have been wronged he can submit a Service complaint. [JSP 831'*Service Complaints, Redress of Individual Grievance*'] and JSP 763 ['*The MOD Harassment Complaints Procedure*'].

3. Why is a well-resourced Service organisation limited to Courts Martial [CM] proceedings, and not utilised for all Service criminal matters?

This point was addressed somewhat obliquely by the JAG some eight years ago [Rant, at 1.09 p.4] and although it appears to represent wholesome support for overhauling the current criminal summary justice system and to remove it from the remit of unqualified staff, the *status quo* remains. If all criminal matters were to be heard in the CM, the Military Court Service [MCS] would obviously face an increased workload. However, the MCS comprises a substantial organisation, with the Directorate of Legal Services [DLS] the RAF alone has 29 different units in the UK and world-wide. Although they do not deal exclusively with service prosecutions, one must ask why, with the resources at their disposal, are not all service criminal prosecutions dealt with in the CM?

Currently the Service Justice System comprises several processes for criminal and disciplinary offences. There is a highly qualified legal staff operating in the CM, there are Commanding

Officers and lower officer-ranks operating the summary process for criminal and minor disciplinary matters and for what may be termed 'personal' failings there is the minor administrative action [MAA] process and major administrative actions. It appears that there are too many processes endeavouring to achieve the same aim.

4. Why were the procedural errors highlighted by the European Court of Human Rights [ECtHR] and corrected in the CM process, not applied to the summary process in the 2016 review?

During the passage of the Armed Forces Act, key aspects of the system were scrutinised and debated and no significant changes to the system were made. [Service Justice Board [SJB] MOD UK, email, 06 July 2017]. Quite why this was cannot be determined, but it is hoped that in the next review, due in 2021, this and other substantial changes will be effected.

5. Why does the MOD maintain a separate, Service Civilian Court [SCC] to deal with civilians subject to Service law? This begs a further question; why is the Forces summary process not applied to civilians also?

The Act does not authorise COs to deal with civilians, and if this is the only reason, then why not. If the MOD consider the summary process is good enough for all servicemen, why can it not be applied to civilians in the service of the Crown? This will not be pursued, as it is only servicemen we are concerned with but it does, if nothing else, raise an interesting question about use of resources.

6. Why does the summary process not allow for the application of the same range of punishments on offenders irrespective of rank?

In the civil process, the same punishments apply to whomsoever is convicted. The only difference might be where an offender could receive a more severe punishment if guilty of a breach of trust or 'should have known better', which is usually applied to the more intelligent, or professional offender, but no punishments are reserved specifically for certain classes of person, but the severity of the sanctions might depend on factors as above. Although this may be a contentious issue, the same rules should apply in Service courts.

There is a great deal to consider on this topic, but it is essential for the Service process to deal with criminal and disciplinary matters in a way that will not attract censure by higher, non-military courts. This is not only to show that a conviction is safe and beyond criticism as far as the offender is concerned, but also that the military have a duty to their servicemen in operating a system which acknowledges the safeguards which the civilian counterpart and his attorney can expect, as far as reasonably possible, in criminal or disciplinary proceedings.

2. **METHODOLOGY**.

The nature of this research is essentially *qualitative*, as we shall be considering a series of documents the main ones being The Manual of Service Law [MSL] and the Armed Forces Act 2006 [The Act] which two volumes comprise the authoritative source on service legislation. In addition, 'Rant on Courts Martial and Service Justice [3rd edition, 2009] [Ed. Blackett, J] principally a reference for officers who deal with Forces justice, comments comprehensively on how ECtHR interventions have shaped the CM procedures although in many cases, not carried through to the summary process.

The Magistrates' Courts Rules 1981 [The Rules] provide the 'Benchmark' against which the Service process was compared, as it is these Rules which ensure, as far as possible, the fair treatment of an accused. The Rules are issued by the High Court therefore represent an unimpeachable authority.

The Questionnaires, surveys and semi-structured Interviews with the Military Court Service [MCS] and Judge Advocate General's Office, together with the documentary evidence, represented good secondary-source analysis, with its cost, time and quality advantages.

There was no ethnographic research, although it would have illuminated any qualitative work, and might have produced some interesting information, but there were disadvantages in that one would have had to [a] find and engage with a large number of servicemen who had been through the summary process and [b] deal with a substantial ethics problem and [c] it would be very time-consuming and [d] one cannot be concerned with historical aspects of the summary process or the effect it had on Servicemen's careers as our remit is to consider the system; how the accused or the offenders were affected might provide scope for further study.

It is a *process* on trial here, so the interviewees might not have been authoritative, accurate and valid critics as would, for example, an officer who had taken a substantial number of summary hearings, either as a Commanding Officer [CO] or as an Accused's Assisting Officer [AAO], and so have an intimate knowledge of the process. As none would have been lawyers [refer the MSL and The Act], it cannot be assumed that they will have an appreciation of the issues this research seeks to address.

Interviewing staff within the Service legal departments raised particular problems because interviewees could realistically do no more than express their departments' policies, nor could they discourse on issues critical of other organisations. As the researcher had an idea of particular issues, and could phrase the questions accordingly, almost inevitably references were to the MSL, The Act or policy. The questionnaires could only, and obviously, address the interviewees' areas of interest and, where there was a particular point to settle, it often went essentially unanswered for reasons as above.

However, the few interviews with those who administer the system and were legally qualified to comment on any shortcomings, did qualify as valid, inductive primary research, so enabling a derivation of sound theory from these sources. Examples are the JAG and the MCS interviews of May and June 2017 respectively.

All other authorities responded to approaches, although some referred to e.g., the MOD contacts for SJS reviews, to the Summary Justice departments and to RAF College Cranwell OACTU who in turn referred to Coningsby and Waddington Legal Support Services, Regional Legal Offices and the Forces Legal Advisor. No surveys were conducted as there were no suitable classes of persons available, and even if there were, there would be difficulties in the number of questions, the way the questions are asked and whether the interviewees felt they could answer honestly or at all in view of their not wanting to be or appear to be voicing an opinion which contradicts Service policy.

The DVD, 'Advice and information for the accused' [produced by the ArmySec-Group@MOD.uk] offers a valuable insight into the hearing of a summary case and from which a number of criticisms can be raised.

The Joint Services Publication [JSP] 833 MOD 10/2008 and Queen's Regulations [QR] s.1027 and Air Publication [AP] 3392 dealt with more aspects of summary justice, MAAs and major administrative actions. Internet postings of Morgan, the National Audit Office, Mwedzi and Brooke-Holland proved useful.

Hence, the majority of the research was of necessity confined to a literature review.

3. LITERATURE REVIEW.

The literature represents a substantial body of information extending to persons subject to Service law in whichever country those persons subject to that law are serving. Although there are two categories of such persons, viz., Service personnel and ex-Service personnel, first category, and civilians subject to Service discipline, second category, we are concerned principally with serving personnel. The literature comprises as follows:

1.   The Service Justice System [SJS] overview is a short brief produced by the Armed Forces Bill team at the Ministry of Defence

[MOD] and although not a detailed overview, does comprise a broad outline of the legal framework within which the Services operate. It points out that the SJS is constructed to provide a mechanism by which those accused of disciplinary offences are dealt with 'fairly, quickly and have a right to appeal against their sentence'.

2.   Armed Forces Act [The Act]. The Act came into effect on 31 October 2009 and represents the first major overhaul of Service law for half a century. In 19 parts, plus 17 schedules, it is a comprehensive document which replaces the old Air Force Act of 1955, the Army Act 1955 and Navy Discipline Act of 1957. Part one lists offences and, understandably, many are exclusive to service personnel such as mutiny, neglect of duty, offences against Service justice and issues relating to ships and aircraft.

3.   Notes to AFA. These form part of essential reading for all purposes related to the AFA but do not form part of the Act and neither have they been endorsed by Parliament. Notwithstanding, of particular interest is the Introduction, the Background and the Overview of the Act and Structure of The Act which provides a concise, albeit short, précis for a casual enquirer into the Act and the remaining 125 pages are an interesting voyage into the SJS which is adequate for all but the most serious student who will have to engage with The Act and its near cousin, the Manual of Service Law.

4.   Rant on The Court Martial and Service Law [third edition] is a comprehensive overview of the Service Justice system. Apart from the chapters setting out most of the Act and various Statutory Instruments and Rules, there is comment by the current Judge Advocate General, HHJ Jeff Blackett which will be liberally quoted as they present valid argument in support of the SJ process and some valid criticism of it and in addition, and most importantly, set out the need for meaningful reform of certain elements of Service justice. Of particular interest is chapter 9 - The Effect of the ECtHR on the SJS, including useful comment on cases which were referred to the ECtHR, and chapter 4 (C) The Summary Hearing. There are many other relevant references to the summary procedure.

5. Manual of Service Law. The MSL is published to provide policy guidance and reference material on the AFA and comprises three volumes and it is volume one, chapters one to 15, as listed above, and Volume two, chapter 27, of which only The Court Guide, and 'The Summary Appeal Court' [SAC] apply. Volume three is a Legal Compendium, then come forms and leaflets.

The MSL runs to 35 chapters, with the sections appropriate to this research amounting to 16 of the chapters, some 600 pages in all. Much of the material needed is buried in various paragraphs within almost all of those volumes, and eliciting the essential information is a substantial task. Chapters relevant to this research are described below.

Chapter 1 is a brief résumé of what the MSL contains.

Chapter 2 'Meaning of Commanding Officer' and how a Serviceman's CO is identified under Defence Council regulations and how an officer, i.e., the holder of the Queen's commission, must be able to identify as being a person's CO, as it is in him the Act invests the power to deal with Servicemen, sub-units, attached personnel and some civilians all of whom are described within the MSL.

Chapter 3 covers jurisdiction and time limits and the bulk of this chapter deals with those who are subject to service law. Summary hearings are heard by a CO, or an empowered subordinate commander, and whose powers depend on the accused's rank. The CO's powers of punishment are set out in Chapter 13 MSL.

Chapter 6. 'Investigation, charging & Mode of trial.' With this research comprising a comparison of the application of summary justice by Magistrates' courts and that as administered by the Services, it is a valuable document and one which will be referred to throughout the dissertation. The chapter aims to be guidance for those responsible for administering discipline, the investigation, selection and charging and deciding on the mode of trial and comprises seven parts, viz., General principles, Offences Overview, Investigation, Offences which can be heard summarily, a section on CM or the SCC [which we do not deal with] and finally Administrative and Welfare responsibilities.

Chapter 7. This is the largest chapter in the MSL, comprising about 200 pages, and covers non-criminal, i.e., disciplinary, offences. There is a substantial number of these offences which are dealt with summarily but are still of importance to this research as is every summary process, and whatever the offence.

Chapter 8. This chapter deals with Service personnel who commit criminal offences some of which can be dealt with summarily and others dealt with summarily but only with permission from higher authority [HA]. Such offences include offences of violence, dishonesty, road traffic offences, section 43 to 48 of the Armed Forces Act 2006 offences – attempting, conspiring, inciting, aiding, abetting, counselling or procuring criminal conduct.

Chapter 9. Summary hearing procedures. This chapter covers a number of points some of which will be addressed in the body of this dissertation.
    Part 1 - Delegations and applications to higher authority [HA];
    Part 2 - Preliminary procedures for a summary nearing;
    Part 3 - General considerations for the summary hearing and preliminary actions;
    Part 4 - Procedures where a charge is denied;
    Part 5 - Where the charge is admitted.
    Parts 6,7,8 and 9 - Post hearing, elections for trial in the CM and activation of a suspended sentence of detention.

Chapter 11. Summary hearing, dealing with evidence. This provides the CO and his staff with the information they need to recognise and deal with issues which may arise during a hearing and to establish the facts and recognise when to seek advice from the Forces Legal Team. This chapter points out that the summary hearing is not a court; it is an inquisitorial process by which the CO endeavours to discover the facts by actively searching for evidence and questioning the witnesses and that ...

'...no rules of evidence as such apply but the principles

ensure both best practice and fairness to the accused ...'.

Chapter 12. Defences, mitigation and criminal responsibility; will be of assistance to the CO and to the accused's assisting officer [AAO].

Chapter 13. Summary hearing, sentencing and punishments sets out the purpose of sentencing and includes punishment, discipline, crime reduction by deterrence, reform and rehabilitation, protection of both the public and Servicemen and reparation and welfare for offenders aged 18 or under. A period in detention aims to do more or less the same as a civilian prison with obvious differences, one being that the maximum term of detention [the Service calls it 'detention'] which can be handed down [with HA] is 90 days in the Military Corrective Training Centre [MCTC] and offenders receive training to improve their physical fitness and Army / Air Force or Navy skills.

Chapter 14. The Summary hearing and sentencing guide; the introduction states ...

'The impartial administration of discipline is essential to the morale and cohesion of a Service unit [and] fairness at summary hearings generates confidence in other aspects of unit management'.

Chapter 15. The review of summary cases by the Defence Council or an officer [The Reviewing Officer [RO]] appointed for this purpose is to see if any grounds exist for referring the summary finding to the Summary Appeal Court [SAC]. It also identifies disciplinary trends and issues to help achieve a 'common approach' to summary findings and punishments. Apart from recording information as above, the RO is not able to take any judicial role, just to refer his reservations to higher authority should he see fit to do so.

Chapter 27. The SAC is established to hear appeals against findings and sentence. It is generally bound by the Rules of Evidence as apply in England and Wales; it also comprises lay members but includes a Judge advocate who oversees the proceedings.

6.   Minor Administrative Action. Minor Administrative Action [MAA – JSP 833]. MAA is action taken to ...

'...rehabilitate, censure or initiate sanctions to correct professional or personal failings ...'.

It is a summary process, and applies the Service Test, i.e., 'have the actions of a Service person adversely affected the efficiency or effectiveness of the Service'. There is a distinction between disciplinary and administrative action in that the former is used where there has been an offence and the latter is used to *'... set straight professional and personal shortcomings ...'* and provision for Major Administrative [disciplinary] Action for more serious, disciplinary offences and which does allow the accused to elect trial in the CM. For MAA there is facility for a review at a level higher than that at which it was initiated, e.g., if initiated by a corporal, the review would normally be by a junior officer. A person who feels that any MAA taken against him is unfair has the right to make a complaint as per JSP 831 or via the MOD's Harassment Complaints Procedure.

7.   Magistrates' Courts Procedure. Magistrates' Courts Procedure and The Magistrates' Courts Rules. The initial training of Magistrates and guidance throughout their careers is overseen by the Judicial College. The process is constantly 'hands-on' to ensure that the Justices are kept abreast of changes in the law and procedure.

8.   DVD - Information for service personnel accused of an offence. This DVD aims to give an overview of the SJS for the accused and is produced with every intention of achieving that aim, and although it is a very professional production it does raise some serious issues not only as regards the summary process, but some matters which do not show the Administration in a particularly good light. These observations will be discussed below and at length.

9. Questionnaires and Semi-structured Interviews with the Military Court

Service [MCS] and Judge Advocate General's Office formed the basis for approaches to those authorities. They were not intended to be completed in isolation, as many side-issues were expected to - and did - arise and which prompted further questions. After each meeting, the responses were written-up and are attached to this dissertation at Annexes A and B.

10. RAF College Cranwell and Command Appointments Law Training. This represents the level of legal knowledge of the Commanding Officers' or, in the alternative, of the junior officers nominated to take summary hearings.

The above represents a substantial volume of information, and it will be seen therefrom that is very little scope for the Service officer to engage with the civil processes as he is only required to operate within the bounds of The Act and the MSL. The CO does however, have a degree of flexibility in how a case is disposed of and he can call on the Forces Legal team for guidance. Likewise, any serviceman facing a summary hearing can elect for trial in the CM or appeal to the SAC if summarily convicted.

4. THE CIVIL LAW - AN OVERVIEW.

In any civilised society, a person who breaks the law can expect sooner or later to engage with its criminal justice system, established to punish those who offend against the criminal laws, formulated to protect the public and its property from the activities of wrongdoers. In the UK the criminal law is established on principles of fairness. Fairness is a subjective concept; what is seen to be fair in one country, or in one organisation or by one person may be regarded as otherwise by another.

For the purposes of this research, the benchmark for 'fairness' in criminal matters will be that as accepted in the UK courts, and as practiced by its law officers and judiciary with the caveat that where the civilian court for any reason fails the 'fairness' test, it will very probably give rise to an appeal against conviction or sentence or both. For current standards in relation to appeals, consider the case of R-v-Johnson [2000] a Canada case.

For the avoidance of doubt, 'fairness' in proceedings shall mean 'reasonable and impartial'; in particular, the right to a fair trial is set out in Article 6 European Convention of Human Rights [ECHR] and is the right to be heard by a competent, independent and impartial tribunal, the right to a public hearing, to be heard within a reasonable time and the right to counsel. In short, and as per the United Nations Universal Declaration of Human Rights. [UNUDHR] ...

'Everyone is entitled in full equality to a fair and public hearing by an independent and impartial tribunal, in the determination of his rights and obligations and of any criminal charge against him.'

A summary hearing before a Magistrate is a judicial process. It aims, should the accused plead not guilty, to give him a reasonable opportunity to plead his case, either acting 'in person' [IP] or, should he so choose, through counsel who will have the necessary skills and knowledge of the law to represent his client and have his case aired fully and competently in court, and those who are judging him are qualified members of the judiciary. In the case of a guilty plea, the same process, or part of it, will deal with sentencing.

His case would normally be heard by Magistrates - [Justices of the Peace [JPs]]. Three usually sit, with one of them, the Chairman, aided by a court clerk, usually a solicitor. However, a district Judge can also sit in the Magistrates' courts. More serious cases are referred to the Crown Court and are dealt with by a Judge. Magistrates and Judges are collectively referred to as 'the Bench'. A Crown Court Judge will be a solicitor or barrister of long-standing, and often, if a barrister, a Queen's Counsel [QC] 'elevated to the Bench' and each will be competent in the field of law in which he practices.

Be the hearing before a Magistrate or Judge, neither will show bias and both will allow the prosecution and the defence to put their respective cases and [usually] without too much interference from the Bench.

The trial, the conduct of the parties, the management of a jury [if there is one] and the presentation of the evidence will be subject to procedures which have been established over many years, governed by rules which each of the advocates and the Magistrates or Judges will be familiar with and which, if they choose to ignore either through ignorance or bloody-mindedness, could well lead to an acquittal, a re-trial or an appeal, which, if based on incorrect procedures during trial or a faulty summing-up, could ultimately be of benefit to the accused.

In the UK, the judiciary, i.e., Judges, or the higher judiciary, being Lords of Appeal, Judges of the Supreme Court or the Court of Session, are highly regarded, and, likewise, solicitors and barristers who work for the Crown Prosecution Service [CPS], overseen by the Director of Public Prosecutions, are separately governed either the Law Society, for solicitors, or the Bar Council, now the Senate of the Inns of Court, for barristers. Barristers and solicitors are Officers of the Supreme Court of Judicature of England and Wales, or of an equivalent authority if in Scotland.

Each of these regulatory bodies is responsible for ensuring the fitness to practice of their separate members. Solicitors who misbehave are removed from the Roll [or probably would not be permitted to renew their practicing certificates] and barristers would be expelled from their Inns of Court [disbarred].

Solicitors and barristers [lawyers is a generic term covering solicitors and barristers and also, confusingly, many unqualified persons who work in the legal profession in some role or other] may be acting for the prosecution on one case and for the defence in another case but are all similarly regulated.

Barristers, usually self-employed, will work through their 'chambers'. Solicitors will be either partners in their law firm or just salaried fee-earners who may, where they do not engage barristers, and if properly trained and authorised, exercise a right of audience as advocates. Those of the lawyers who fail to make the grade in their court work will not usually have a long career in advocacy.

So much for criminal law; for disciplinary, i.e., non-criminal behaviour, in cases where a worker is to be disciplined for misbehaving, or is incompetent or commits a breach of his contract of employment, there are various safeguards to ensure that any disciplinary action taken by an employer will conform to certain employment laws or Trades Union codes of practice. These give the worker protection against, for example, a tyrannical boss who may seek to sack an employee for anything other than legitimate reasons. Similarly, the rules set out the terms of compensation for those who have been made redundant.

Employment courts - Employment Tribunals - formerly Industrial Tribunals - and the Employment Appeal Tribunal [EAT], a superior court of record, are set up to deal with issues arising out of employer / employee disputes. In each case, hearings are managed and regulated by professionals who will usually specialise in employment work.

It will be seen from the foregoing, that whether a matter is dealt with under criminal law, or is a discipline matter and dealt with under employment law, there are bodies established to ensure that, whatever the issues within those two disciplines, hearings are conducted by professional people, overseen by higher authorities to ensure in each case that justice is done and is at all stages applied fairly.

Notwithstanding, there is a substantial body of persons to whom the above does not apply. These are members of H.M. Armed Forces.

5. MILITARY DISCIPLINE.

[A] A short history

Things *were* tough in the military. '*Soldiers must fear their officers more than they fear the enemy* ' [Frederick the Great, King of Prussia 1712 – 1786]. Whether he was right or wrong, he certainly had some notable military victories under his belt.

The application of discipline in the English Navy and the British Army up to nineteenth century was arbitrary and brutal and often on the orders of an officer or NCO without any kind of trial, so much so that, as far as the Navy was concerned, the 17th Century Rump Parliament was moved to regulate Navy discipline and passed the Laws of War and Ordinances of the Sea Act. [Rodger, 2004]

Later 'The Articles of War', it remained in force until the Naval Discipline Act [NDA] 1866. To the sailor this meant petty courts-martial to try offences and a conviction meant various punishments could be administered, from hanging, flogging or 'flogging round the fleet' and keel-hauling. Between 1649 and 1660 only two sailors were hanged afloat, one a seaman and the other a Captain for murdering one of his men. [Rodger, ibid]

Hanging was usually reserved for mutiny, treason or desertion; as to flogging, a Captain could only legitimately order twelve lashes. Any more than twelve would have to be a sentence passed in the CM but the Captain's limit was often exceeded without comment from the Admiralty. Overly brutal behaviour by a Captain could, in extreme circumstances, lead to bloody mutiny such as that of Captain Pigot's frigate HM *'Hermione'* in 1797. [Rodger, ibid]

The NDA also removed the duty of the JAG to prosecute cases, but he retained the duty of supervising prosecutions after the Lewis Committee report of 1946 when the Army Act had all uniformed prosecutors join the Army Legal Service. The RAF adopted the Army disciplinary code and the role of the JAG then extended to the RAF. [Rant,1.19]

Navy discipline was regarded as being somewhat milder than that of the Army and even as late as the mid-nineteenth century, soldiers were viciously flogged for their misdemeanours. Apart from a flogging, a deserter could be branded and tattooed with a 'D'; a person of bad character could be branded with 'BC'. [Featherstone 1966] Featherstone again;
'English literature gives sparse treatment to the British

soldier, with the possible exception of Shakespeare's 'King Henry V' or Kipling's 'Barrack Room Ballads' or his 'Soldiers Three'.

Wellington [Duke of] opposed pay rises for his men and his sole recipe for discipline was flogging and death. To a Royal Commission he was reported as saying ...

> *'I have no idea of any great effect being produced on British soldiers by anything but the fear of immediate corporal punishment.' And later ' ...they are the scum of the earth; English soldiers are fellows who have all enlisted for drink – that is the plain fact, they have all enlisted for drink... '*

> And it has been said that ' ... *Kipling's writings' moulded a whole generation of young Englishmen who rose up in their thousands in 1914 and sacrificed themselves in the image that he had created...'.* [Featherstone, ibid]

Books about WW1 illustrate how wretched the conditions were for the British soldier and just how harsh was the punishment for, e.g., losing a rifle or apparently deserting, when in fact the individuals were frequently far from the cowards they were accused of being, and very often subjected to the ultimate penalty. Sassoon's *Memoirs of an Infantry Officer*, and much of WW1 poetry, describe well the injustices perpetrated during that war.

Collie, In a Times report [4 June 1914, reproduced 2017] stated that ...

> ' *...most, if not all, cases of neurasthenia were as a result of 'shell-shock' and must on no account be supposed that it was a fraud. It was not malingering; it was not wicked self-deception and above all it was not cowardice. It was a real disease found among men remarkable for their bravery, daring, and initiative and they were not cowards ...'*

Regrettably, the message did not always filter through to the front-line commanders before they jumped to conclusions regarding the troops who may have been charged with cowardice *inter alia.*

So bad were the conditions under which the soldiers fought and lived in WW1, and so bad was the French soldiers' treatment by their officers, that the French army at Verdun mutinied, but Marshal Pétain managed to rally his troops, with the near-mutiny hushed up, or as good as. [Gavin]

Fair or otherwise, punishments were effected after the most cursory of hearings, if there was any hearing. These days however, it is essential for the processes of law to be seen to be fair before any form of punishment can be administered. It might be apt here to consider how the generals, from their relatively comfortable billets, issued orders such as those to the airmen who were forbidden to carry parachutes in their flimsy machines as the generals thought that the crews would bale out of the aircraft to avoid engaging with the enemy; or orders to the front-line troops in their appalling living conditions such as those to the 419 Field Company Royal Engineers on a point of discipline emphasising the necessity for the men to 'properly salute their officers'; [Van Emden 2017] or another order stating that due to a shortage of fat 'men were allowed to dip their bread on the bacon fat on one side only.' [Van Emden Ibid] They had been warned!

All this when men were drowning in the mud-pools of France.

[B] The 21st century.

The civilian UK courts lay down strict rules and engage professionals in its administration of justice. On the other hand, the Serviceman's criminal [and disciplinary] summary cases are heard entirely by lay-persons. It begs the question; if the civil authorities see fit to have in place procedures and safeguards overseen by highly qualified, professional legal staff, to ensure that the accused was afforded every assistance to put his case, why do the same conditions not apply to H.M. Forces summary justice thereby complying with inter alia, Article 6 ECHR?

All the evidence suggests that the contrary applies; that no legally qualified personnel are engaged in the hearing of summary cases, yet the punishments have the same serious consequences for the offender as apply in the civil courts.

There can be no argument that discipline in HM Forces is, of necessity, far removed from that which applies to civilians. However, there are some civilians to whom military law does apply, and those are members of specific organisations such as the NAAFI, Service Children's Education, the Services Sound and Vision Corporation [SSVC], Soldiers Sailors and Air Forces Association [SSAFA] and those who are serving overseas and persons residing or staying with, a person subject to Service law [see the case of Martin-v-UK covered in this dissertation] and Contractors on Deployed Operations [CODO].

Cases concerning them would be a CM process, by the Service Civilian Court [SCC] established for that very purpose, but it becomes difficult to determine why there should be this distinction. Apart from the obvious point that the serviceman wears a uniform, why is the Service summary process deemed inadequate for the civilians, and a separate court established exclusively for dealing with them?

As mooted above, Servicemen have to maintain an overall higher standard of discipline than that expected of other members of society, and there is an additional range of offences which apply to them. They have to obey orders without question; they live in very close proximity to their peers, to their NCOs and sometimes to their officers, where any kind of criminal activity or lack of discipline, if not checked, can undermine the effectiveness of their units. They must trust implicitly the people with whom they fight, sail and fly, but that does not mean that offenders must be subject to a tribunal which dispenses what could be regarded as 'second-rate' justice.

The Act and the MSL govern their behaviour and it is perhaps worthy of note that MSL chapter seven, which deals with non-criminal conduct [disciplinary] offences, is the largest chapter in the MSL. It runs to 57 sections and most of these offences can be dealt with summarily and apply whether the military unit is serving in the UK or overseas but subject always to certain protocols such as Status of Forces Agreements [SOFA] or any Memoranda of Understanding [MOU] which may be applied by certain governments or regimes where the Services operate.

There is nothing set out in the processes outlined which would raise any concern in the servicemen who may at one time or another face a summary hearing, and nor would a CO, tasked with taking a summary hearing, have any reservations about his authority to fulfil his role in the process; we know his authority arises out of the Act and the MSL. The information available to him in these two volumes is all he needs to exercise his powers to convict and punish.

At some stage he will, as a unit CO, have had some instruction on how such a hearing should be conducted. His training would introduce him to the SJS and how to manage a summary hearing. [The Act pt. 6 Ch.1 and the MSL Chapters 11, 12 & 13 *'Summary Hearing - Dealing with Evidence, Defences etc.* and *Summary Hearing, Sentencing and Punishments.*]

As this research is concerned with the delivery of summary justice in Her Majesty's Armed Forces and the question 'is it fair' [fair, that is, on the accused], we can now consider some other criticisms of the Service justice process.

[C] Kangaroo Courts?

A 2012 report was produced by an anonymous, but serving, Army officer for the Defence Select Committee [DSC] as evidence for its investigation into how the service handles complaints and discipline. Members of Parliament who comprise the DSC were expected to produce their findings a year after that report. However, the only 2013 report of any significance, as far as legal issues are concerned, is the *'UK Armed Forces Personnel and the Legal Framework for Future Operations, Twelfth Report of Session'* printed on 26 March 2013, and it concentrated on Iraq Historical Allegations Team [IHAT] and the procedures regarding the prosecution of the alleged offenders. As no other relevant report has been unearthed, it is more than likely that the 2012 report was in fact a British Armed Forces Federation [BAFF] paper sent on the 25th February 2013 to the DSC. N.B.; numerous attempts were made to contact the BAFF but regrettably, they failed to respond.

The report or paper was picked up by Kris Jepson, a journalist, and aired on Channel 4 news. The author, his rank and his job in the Army unknown, averred that Army discipline was ...

> '...rarely transparent or accountable, was frequently unlawful in the way it handles complaints and discipline...'

... and he called for an overhaul of an Army procedure [then] known as Army General Administrative Instruction 67 [AGAI 67] - now believed to have been superseded by other administrative actions. These concerns were reflected by Rojas [2012] who added that the Ministry of Defence had ignored the lessons of Deepcut, the Surrey barracks where four recruits died amid claims of a culture of bullying.

The Jepson report made the following specific charges; no safeguards to protect junior personnel from the chain of command; nothing to prevent dishonest commanders from pursuing vendettas against those working under them; service lawyers questioned the legality of using the system; it breached Article 6 of the European Convention on Human Rights [ECHR]; equivalent civilian disciplinary systems are governed by ACAS rules. It concluded that the AGAI 67 should be rewritten. It is regrettable that the officer concerned cannot be identified but such allegations cannot just be ignored without enquiry especially as they seem to support similar criticisms from other sources referred to here.

There are currently two administrative actions, namely Minor Administrative Action [MAA] and the Major Administrative Action and it is important to make the distinction, not least because it will be proposed that both be developed as suitable alternatives to certain aspects of the CO's summary court. An MAA is intended to deal with professional and personal shortcomings, and in many cases the outcome is an order to attend further training or some other modest punishment. Full information is available in JSP 833.

The more serious offences are dealt with by a Major

[disciplinary] action and can be dealt with either via a summary hearing or in the CM if the transgressor so chooses. Punishments can be applied.

Annex C sets out information on the MAA and the Major action and is useful to see the form and extent of the sanctions available. These Actions represent another element of the summary justice process.

The summary court make-up was alluded to in the 2012 report as not being compliant with Article 6 [ECHR] as, inter alia, the CO acts as Judge, prosecutor and jury. One can take judicial notice of the fact that in any UK court [with very few exceptions] these three roles are taken by three different people. There is another factor; in view of the nature of the Forces, and their being accommodated within a single unit or camp, it is likely that the CO, the accused and the accused's assisting officer [AAO] will all know each other in their various working capacities. Hence the question as to independence and impartiality of that 'tribunal' is a reasonable point to address.

It was the Grieves case [2003, ECHR 57067/00 [Rant 1.17 p6] where the ECtHR found that, to have serving officers as Judge advocates in the CM was a breach of Article 6 [right to fair trial] and yet it is serving officers who hear summary cases. There can only be a very thin line which distinguishes the two. In view of the above, the summary process, is effectively a CO's 'court'.

If an AAO planned, prior to the commencement of a summary hearing and running the risk of being criticised as 'playing the lawyer', to refer the CO to Article 6, the CO, who would very probably be unfamiliar with the Article, would have a number of choices, viz., [a] ignore it, [b] refer to the Forces Legal Team for guidance on how to proceed or [c] proceed with the hearing regardless on the basis that the offender could appeal the conviction in the SAC or [d] suggest to the AAO or the accused that he just applies for trial in the CM.

However, this is not an entirely satisfactory way to proceed as the accused is entitled to a fair hearing be it before a summary 'tribunal' or in the CM and to force him to undergo what could be a series of unnecessary processes could be stressful and protracted, and further, the accused might be inclined to just want to get it all over with sooner rather than later. This was a view aired in the Jepson report and is addressed again below.

Another consideration is that the Forces do not regard the summary hearing as being a court and might therefore deny that Article 6 applies. However, the UNUDHR does not mention 'courts' but 'tribunals', [Doebbler 2006] which are defined as being...

> '...a body outside the hierarchy of the courts with administrative or judicial functions exercising an independent jurisdiction ...'

- which is a more than adequate description of a summary hearing.

It is not for the CO to involve himself in distinguishing between courts and tribunals, or to make a determination thereon or to engage in debate on Article 6, as to do so he could be acting *ultra vires*. Nevertheless, he will exercise his authority under the Act knowing that, if the accused is so determined, he can pursue the matter as set out above. This throws up another example of the deficiencies in the summary process in that there is no equivalent of an 'in chambers' conference between prosecution, defence and Judge to discuss this kind [or any kind] of point; indeed, technically, no such personages exist, and with no lawyers involved at the hearing stage, such a proposition would very probably not occur to the parties concerned.

Those facing a summary hearing are, if the AAO is doing his job, advised of their rights to opt for court martial, but the report claims that the circumstances of the accused *vis-à-vis* the command chain, and with the assistance of an unqualified AAO, who may himself be under some pressure to have the case dealt with, and the need felt by the accused *et al* to get the matter over with, means any subtle, if not direct pressure to do so does not offer a genuinely free choice. The MOD counter this allegation with the defence that soldiers '... *make informed decisions to opt for summary hearings ...*'. That might be the case. Or it might not.

The Jepson Report made other allegations such as the summary process being used to turn accused away from the CM option; to cover-up misconduct by 'favoured' personnel by 'going through the motions of prosecution, with acquittal pre-determined, and to mislead servicemen on the implications of a guilty finding against them. These are quite serious allegations, and, to be fair, if this were found to be the case, then the MOD should have dealt with it, or, in the alternative, be planning to deal with it, as part of the forthcoming 2021 Review.

It alleges, too, that the conviction rate in summary hearings is 90 per cent although the JAG's office suggests that it is as high as 95% [interview, JAG 30/05/201730 May 2017] compared to that of 50% in the CM. A Colonel [same report] at a meeting at the Joint Services Command and Staff College [JSCSC] is reported as saying...

> '...If soldiers knew about the difference in conviction rate, they would never elect for summary hearing ... and if they were to, it would 'break' the courts martial system ...'.

The JAG's office agrees that there is a real possibility of 'straining' the system, but not breaking it. [May 30th 2017 interview]. It is better that the SPA do not have to face either of those options unless they plan to deal with all criminal hearings in the first instance in the CM and make adequate provision for it. The SPA website [Ministry of Defence Service Prosecuting Authority' at 'About' states:-

> '...No prosecution authority can predict the level of crime or the volume of cases which will be referred to it in a given year. In the case of the SPA there are clearly risks in terms of case-flow. It is conceivable that the changes made by the Act [Armed Forces Act 2006] may see a reduction in summary dealing, and a higher volume of cases being referred to the SPA. Where COs follow proper procedure, are alert to their responsibilities, and are able to instil trust in those under command, summary dealing, or minor administrative action, can still be both an effective and appropriate manner of dealing with less serious criminal or

disciplinary offences. Reducing delay is a key aim of the Service Justice System. It remains the intention that Service law should reflect the provisions of the civilian justice system as far as it is sensible and practical to do so. This involves recognition of the need to sustain Service ethos and discipline. Attention to detail in preserving the best and changing those procedures which do not serve us well, will be another target of our attention in the years ahead ...'.

The Jepson article concludes ...

'... I would argue that the military should be transparent, accountable and lawful - and that at present it is rarely transparent or accountable and frequently unlawful. While a parallel legal system is necessary to satisfy the requirements of the Services' unique role [the application of lethal force on behalf of the nation] and its potentially expeditionary nature, the SJS which administers this should be both independent and professional...'

The Services Complaints Commissioner [SCC] [since the 2015 the Armed Forces [Service Complaints and Financial Assistance Commissioner] Act, the Service Complaints Ombudsman - effective 1 January 2016, a post currently filled by Nicola Williams] is appropriate here as the MAA permits a person to take his case to this level. However, Jepson alleges that the Army is ...

'...willing to cover-up mistakes, bully personnel, victimise those who complain, and harass those who are perceived to be 'rocking the boat', in order to protect the power and prestige of the chain of command ...'.

As farfetched as this might appear, the system might be broken in the sense that it invests too much power and discretion in the CO and subordinates acting under his authority, in a procedure which bears little resemblance to any legal process under the civil law, but with outcomes just as serious for the offender. Whether the appointment of the Service Ombudsman will signal an improvement in the situation remains to be seen.

So, how is it that these allegations are levelled against a system set up by the MOD, ergo HM Government, and managed by senior officers? There can be a number or reasons, one possibly being that inadequate pressure is being applied to change it, or the allegations are unjustified. It appears thus far that the latter may not be the fairer assessment.

[D] Who are we dealing with?

Empirical evidence suggests that some of the less endearing aspects of the SJS explored thus far and with respect to the 'kangaroo courts' issue, are in all probability unlikely to arise too often but cannot be ignored as a valid topic to discuss. However, one important factor is the nature of the serviceman and how the SJS has in place procedures to cope with those of them who might for any one of a number of reasons be regarded as 'vulnerable' and whether a Commanding Officer has addressed this issue during his own training and introduction to the system.

Although few servicemen, as with the UK population, have border-line mental and/or behavioural issues, anything beyond border-line is almost certainly going to mean they fail their basic training if indeed they are accepted in the first place.

The UK armed forces comprise some 152,000 regular, full-time, trained personnel in the Army, the Royal Navy and the Royal Air Force [MOD - UK *Armed Forces Monthly Service Personnel Statistics* [June 2017] [AFMSPS]]. They serve in a dozen or so overseas military installations, plus the UK. Over the year to December 2016, there were 10,000 fewer serving personnel than the previous year; 2,000 more servicemen left the forces than joined. The Army is failing to recruit its target of 82,000 and current strength is only 78,410 [Ibid].

The youngest age for joining HM Forces is 16 years and the recruits can sign on for a certain minimum period but a 'term of engagement' does not start running until that person is 18, nor can they take part in operations, e.g., serve in areas of conflict, until that age. The length of service required before the MOD will accept a resignation is four years. [Ibid]. However, certain easier options for termination apply to new recruits still undergoing induction and initial trade-training.

Not one of the three forces has recently achieved its recruiting target and the current deficit against planned [needed] personnel seems, at 4.5%, to be modest enough, but in real terms it means there is a shortage of personnel to man the new aircraft carriers, HMS Queen Elizabeth and HMS Prince of Wales, and pilots to fly the new F35 Lightning stealth jets. [National Audit Office – Sir Amyas Morse 2017]. In April 2017 it was announced by the MOD that shortfalls will be partially made up by assigning a contingent of 200 Royal Marines to the carriers when they come into service.

Although the standard of education in literacy and numeracy for Army applicants is not expected to be high, although some older applicants are well-qualified some with degrees, ONCs or City & Guilds qualifications. Four percent of recruits attain level two, and 39% have the literacy level of an eleven year-old.

Some servicemen who go into service detention are unable to read properly but the Military Corrective Training Centre [MCTC] assesses all servicemen under sentence and teaches them to a standard required of them to more effectively carry out their respective roles, and thereby aims to return them to duty in many cases better qualified than when they were checked into the MCTC. [JAG's office, June 2017].

Even in the first world war, Sassoon [Memoirs of an Infantry Officer] talks of some of his men displaying an 'adolescent simplicity' which, added to the generally appalling conditions they endured, made some of his men easy targets for an uncaring NCO or officer.

It is interesting to look at the Times News Review of 6 June 2016 *'Deceit, narcissism and chaos from the charmer who trashed Britain'* - a Tom Bower article sub-titled *'We fell for the oily promises, but his decade of power left our military in tatters and children unemployable .. by Blair's calamitous mixture of incompetence and disdain'*. One could then argue that, if indeed the youth of today was let down by the various policies of Blair's government, the young recruits should be assisted in every way to get through their basic training and to improve their literacy and numeracy levels. In fact, they are.

There is an important issue here; one might seriously question whether recruits who are so ill-equipped with literacy and numeracy skills, are either 'vulnerable' or might be regarded as having 'learning difficulties' and so require careful handling. This will be addressed more fully infra. The Services [the Army in particular] aims to educate all recruits to GCSE level three within three years of joining [Ashcroft, ibid] so clearly the Forces are aware of a literacy and numeracy problem and credit is due to them for their dealing with it.

It may be that such limited educational achievements indicate some other, and perhaps more serious, underlying problems, and whether the Services also appreciate this and address it is a moot point. It is unlikely that such an individual would not be deselected before his recruiting process were completed. If not, then this topic could be real problem for any prosecuting authority, and not just that of the Services.

Gibb and Ames [2017] when discussing the conviction of Damon Smith, jailed for bomb-making [he placed his 'viable' home-made device on the London Underground during rush hour] quote Marie Bourke as saying ...

> ' ... A rise in defendants relying on evidence of their learning difficulties or other mental-health issues is crucial in ensuring that they receive the appropriate sentence ...'

Although not particularly well expressed, the meaning seems clear. The article adds ...

> '... Judges have been encouraged to educate themselves so that they have more empathy and consideration of an individual's circumstances...'

Dr Clare Allely, lecturer in psychology, university of Salford, an expert in autism in the criminal justice system ...

'...There is no defence of 'autism' in this country although it, as with other mental disorders, could be a mitigating factor...'.

This seems to imply that there might be such a defence in other countries. This might be a future research topic. Notwithstanding, some autism sufferers are highly intelligent and articulate, *but it does not follow that they understand the social rules* [Allely, ibid] and it is suggested in the Gibb article that Smith's interest in weaponry *'might have been connected to his condition'*, another Allely point. She adds ...

'...People with autism may not read 'signals' and may think a woman is encouraging them and before you know it you have a serious sexual assault ...'

The implications are clear. It takes skill to identify in any individual potential or actual issues such as this, unless the offence or the behaviour of the accused was 'gross and obvious' and which indicated some underlying abnormality of mind, in which case the accused would be a natural candidate for a hearing in the CM, if not destined for the hospital, but either way, the CO could pass the case on for trial in the CM if there is the least suspicion of such an issue. The worst outcome would be if he were to deal with it summarily without knowing, or recognising but ignoring, the symptoms.

Consider principles of responsivity Nee [2012];

1. Risk principle: Match the level of service to the offender's risk to re-offend;

2. Need principle: Assess criminogenic needs and target them in treatment;

3. Maximize the offender's ability to learn from a rehabilitative intervention by providing cognitive behavioural treatment and tailoring the intervention to the learning style, motivation, abilities and strengths of the offender.

Although aimed at ages of seven and upward, this might make

interesting reading for policy-makers in dealing with the under-18s who have taken the major step of joining the Armed Forces. This is way beyond the knowledge of a CO, but the question is not this, but rather, will issues such as this be recognised. One hopes that it will never arise in this context, and in any event the number who might fall into this category would be relatively few.

The whole topic of young recruits or youth generally and their treatment by the criminal justice system is too vast a subject to cover in this dissertation but should be a consideration in the context of whether a CO can recognise a circumstance or situation and act accordingly.

Ashcroft, [ibid] states that one third of applicants who join the military fail to complete basic training and half of all servicemen who do join serve less than six years. There may, then, be something in the discipline argument that makes them decide that it is 'too tough'. There are surveys available on this, and the JAG's office [June 2017] suggests that it may relate to a disciplined life-style, but this is another angle worthy of further study. Reasons for leaving include:- have done enough time in uniform, do not like the life and/or have family obligations. [ibid].

These are very probably the ones who might, with careful handling, be convinced that a Service career is for them, but to be treated by a CO who is not sensitive to the effect of summary proceedings on the younger recruits under his command, or perhaps by NCO's in MAA proceedings, and so feeling he has been badly treated could be a factor on his deciding to leave even before his basic training is complete, or, perhaps worse for the Service, once fully trained.

A formal and intimidating summary hearing process, fair or otherwise, or even the necessity of the proceedings, for what might in reality have been a fairly innocuous offence against service discipline or a minor criminal matter, may seriously affect the younger, more vulnerable recruit's determination to remain in the forces. However, where an offence has been committed some kind of formal process is inevitable.

Especially at risk are those at a very early stage in their training, who may be away from home for the first time and where even a minor setback makes them likely to apply for discharge, as evidenced by the recent TV programmes following new recruits and which provided ample evidence of this. There is also the parent-input, as enunciated by Kelsall [2017] of *UK Veterans One Voice,* and whose members were advising their own children not to join-up to become scapegoats, referring to the 'Marine A' case and IHAT and those who do sign-on regardless but then experience problems, may come under parental pressure to quit.

Another issue arises here; the needs of young offenders should be addressed as they are in the civil courts. They can be accompanied by a 'responsible adult', and this applies whether or not they appear mature enough to see things through on their own. This is for a number of reasons, including that they are less responsible for their actions than adults, even though some might be very 'street wise'.

Unfortunately, the Service process does not allow for e.g., a 'McKenzie friend' to sit with the accused and quietly reassure him but having no role in the proceedings. In civil courts, such a person is allowed with any accused regardless of his age, if the accused so chooses.

In cases where disciplinary and minor criminal offences are dealt with by summary proceedings, and where all personnel involved are lay-persons, will they be able to appreciate all the various issues, where applicable, as described above? The answer is very probably not, and where an accused does fall into any of the categories, he has a right to have them taken into account by his CO or, in the case of a minor administrative action [MAA], by his senior NCO's, or otherwise by the MAA reviewing officer.

Empirical evidence suggests that at whatever stage a recruit decides he wants to discontinue his career, any incident will be seized upon, but a CO has a unique opportunity to show compassion, to take an interest in his men and to generally engage with them to a far greater degree than would normally present itself in the normal course of events. He can ensure thereby that the outcome of any proceedings can be of a more constructive determination to benefit the offender rather than being purely punitive.

The point of considering the individuals' respective capacities is that it is a feature of the administration of civil justice and if this is an issue which a CO is not equipped to deal with in his capacity as administering summary justice, then, ergo, justice will not be done. To put this into perspective, it is not the fault of the CO that he fails to recognise a duty to the accused, even though he may in every other respect be performing in accordance with The Act, and will not be expected to delve into every aspect of an accused's background, educational achievements or medical history, and where the justice is to be dispensed without undue delay, there would be no time for such protracted research into an accused's history.

It is worth noting that any civilian defence lawyer would indeed make inquiry into his client's background, but the obvious point here is, with the CO acting in several capacities, which does he feel is the most important? This is of course, a rhetorical question but does again raise the issue of Article 6 ECHR.

The law is duty bound to consider the capacity of the accused, and this requires greater skill and knowledge than a CO is required to display, and touches on whether the necessary components of an offence, viz., the *actus reus,* and more particularly, the *mens rea,* the guilty mind or criminal intention. For an offence to have been committed there must be a coincidence of both of these elements, i.e., *the act* and *the intent* [absolute liability offences excepted]. Where the prosecution will endeavour to demolish any defence based on either of these elements, and how this will apply where the Judge, jury and inquisitor is vested in the same person, is difficult to comprehend.

[E] The Service Summary Hearings.

A Service summary hearing is well illustrated by a DVD

produced by the SJS as an aid for the accused and for the AAO. It is a useful tool for this research, as it also highlights several problems.

It opens with the Introduction, then Guide for Summary Hearing, Guide for Court Martial [which will not be addressed] then a SJS Overview for use by those briefing on Service Justice. The scenario is a young soldier [Martin] who assaults a fellow soldier who was being a bit of a nuisance; a punch causes ABH. Martin has a few problems; mother ill with cancer; a young sister at home and for whom he feels responsible.

Looking at the DVD;

Introduction; duration 1 minute 16 seconds.

Opens with the accused standing in front of his CO, a Colonel, with his
AAO, an officer, and three other persons. A total of six persons in the
office. Point; the numbers could be somewhat overwhelming, and the
roles of those present was not explained to the accused.

The commentary explains that the process is correct and 'in accordance with the law'. Point; this is somewhat ambiguous; it does not state which law, but, as already intimated, it would be reasonable to assume that the
commentator is referring to the Act and the MSL; this point should be made clear. The brevity of the introduction is also of some concern.

Guide for Summary Hearing; duration 2 minutes 12 seconds

States that the accused's CO has conduct of the proceedings [unless delegated to another officer] and the hearing is normally held in the CO's office. Point; the CO is known to the accused and will therefore already be familiar with the accused's service record, good or bad or good and bad.

Who's Who at Summary Hearing. The commentary explains who

is who viz., the accused; the AAO; his role is explained. However, the instructions for the AAO's duties is a seven-page brief in the MSL. Point: the explanation in the DVD takes less than one minute.

CO; ensures that the accused has had at least 24 hours to 'read the papers'. In a finding of guilt, or in the case of a guilty plea, the CO - using the guide to punishment - will sentence the accused, after any plea in mitigation is heard.

The Adjutant; there to record what takes place and to ensure that the paperwork is filled in correctly.

The accused's Company Commander or other officer may be there to provide evidence of character in the event of a finding of guilt or a guilty plea.

Regimental Sergeant Major [RSM]; runs the hearing 'on behalf of the CO' and helps the proceedings go smoothly. Point; does not explain what *'runs the hearing on behalf of the CO and helps the proceedings go smoothly'* means. This is somewhat confusing as the CO has full control of the hearing at all times.

The Accused's Story; 9 minutes 27 seconds.

The accused tells his story to the camera and admits that he did it' "Yeah, I hit him". Then a cut back to the CO who reads the charge as being *"That you on the 14 June 2008 committed a civil offence contrary to s. 42 of the AFA that is to say assault occasioning actual bodily harm contrary to s. 47 of the Offences against the Person Act 1861".* [MSL Chapter 8 pp. 1-8-6 to 1-8-17 cover offences of violence; under this section, it has to be an offence which is punishable by law in England and Wales [which it is] or if done in E & W would be so punishable]. Point; s.42 comes under criminal conduct [although assault can also be a civil offence of tort] and the specimen charge should have been *'Committing a criminal-conduct offence contrary to section 42 of the Armed Forces Act 2006 namely section 47 of the Offences Against The Person Act 1861 namely assault occasioning actual bodily harm'* and then the details such as *AB on [date] assaulted CD thereby occasioning actual bodily harm'.*

The CO can hear this charge but only with permission of higher authority [HA] which he says that he has. The offence, according to the OAPA 1861, carries a term of imprisonment not exceeding 5 years; however, the CO is limited in that the maximum he can 'hand down' with his HA is 90 days detention.

There follows an accused's interview with the AAO; it is reasonable enough but there is still a degree of 'he is an officer' and the accused will no doubt feel [and as the interview progressed it becomes obvious] that the accused was not able to **fully and robustly** express his feelings about the incident. At the hearing; the CO adds, after stating that the accused had been before him before on the same charge, that the next incident will be heard in CM then he goes on to say, " *...and it will be a discharge ... "*. Point; It is wrong, and unethical, to 'determine' the outcome of a higher court's findings or sentence; the first depends on the facts of the case presented to THAT court, and the second is the prerogative of the court concerned to determine sentence and not for a 'lower' authority to guess.

The AAO's story; his role is to;
a. Explain process to accused; advise on his rights and availability of legal advice;
b. Take him through relevant parts of the CJS;
c. Keep discussions confidential;
d. Explain the options;
e. Give information, not orders;
f. Prepare witness questions;
g. Get character witnesses;
h. Draft a plea in mitigation;
i. Discuss the appeal options and immediate actions after the case has been heard.

The burden on the AAO is quite substantial bearing in mind he is unlikely to be experienced in the law and may well have been chosen by the accused as a friend or work colleague. In view of the seriousness of a conviction, and that the offender may not want to pursue it to an appeal [or elect trial in the CM] it seems unfair not to allow an accused proper legal representation at the 'court' / 'tribunal' of first instance. The DVD is a professional production, but with a little more thought it could be of greater assistance to the accused. Firstly, it is too short to be of real benefit to the accused and the AAO and as a result, it throws back onto them the need to refer to The Act and [in this particular case] the MSL which sets out the full information the AAO really needs to assimilate.

It would have been useful for the AAO to have looked at the details of how the offence is comprised - the ingredients - as set out in Chapter 8 MSL [Criminal Conduct Offences; violence 1-8-6 to 1-8-17] then to consider the defences, mitigation and criminal responsibility as in Chapter 9 MSL. A few of the twelve pages would be of interest in this case. Bearing in mind the above, had at some stage a lawyer been brought into the equation, he could have gone over the chapters 8 and 9 to pick up on a number of issues which were not addressed in the DVD and, had they been, would have offered valuable assistance in, if not a defence, a far better presentation of the facts to the court and so mitigating the degree of the accused's responsibility. In this case there was no suggestion of mental illness but even a minor level of provocation [and perhaps temporary loss of control at the moment the assault took place] could possibly be pleaded and of value to the accused's case.

If there were any questions of the accused's fitness to face a summary [or any] hearing, the AAO ought to be aware of it, but in such cases, where appropriate, the Armed Forces [Unfitness to Stand Trial and Insanity] Regulations 2009 would apply. Clearly, we cannot be looking at the M'Naghten Rules [insanity] as if there were any question of insanity, it would have doubtless been obvious long before the accused got past the first recruiting interview, or completed basic training. One hopes.

It is unfortunate that the final DVD production did not deal with a number of the above points, which should have been obvious to a trained lawyer. In addition, a discussion between a legal advisor, assuming at some stage such a person were consulted, and the accused and the AAO, might have been a worthwhile element to include in the DVD and perhaps, in this case, appropriate.

In summary, the DVD, probably the only medium which would be easy for the accused to assimilate, could have been a better production to show how the AAO could have taken into account all the circumstances surrounding the case and to do an overall better job for the accused. He is there to help the accused, and with a modestly longer presentation, more could be done to reflect the AAO's role as he is the only representation the accused is likely to have at the summary hearing. As mooted above, the procedure could have been more tightly controlled so leaving the professional viewer with a more satisfactory impression that the accused was better served. It might have been equally useful for all the other persons who were to be present at the hearing, the Co included.

It is surprising that, over the nine-or-so years since this DVD was produced, it has not been updated to take into account the comments of an experienced criminal lawyer. This DVD is, in many cases, the only instruction that Servicemen under training receive on Service law, and empirical evidence shows that the overall impression of recruits who saw this DVD was that they should [a] not drink and [b] not punch people. Which is fair enough, but some kind of discussion after the DVD had been shown might have been useful.

[F] Forces' officers – 'legal' training.

One group of people who cannot be criticised for their role in the Service summary justice process, is the officers tasked with its delivery. All officers will receive basic instruction in Service law during initial training at RAF College Cranwell, the Royal Military Academy, Sandhurst or the Britannia Royal Naval College, Dartmouth. Later in their careers when they study for their promotion exams, they will also consider the SJS. Officers who take up command posts, can do so with little or no further training, their authority to conduct summary hearings and award sanctions deriving from The Act. In each case, however, they will have been required to study only the main texts relating to that law, viz., the Act and the MSL and associated JSP's. They might, however, be interested in attending as an observer at least one civil trial, i.e., one at a Crown court.

Further, the CO can quite legitimately nominate a junior officer to conduct a summary hearing on his behalf, and that could be a Flight Lieutenant, or other service equivalent who may have no more than a basic knowledge, and probably little or no experience in hearing cases. He will not necessarily be required to have any greater knowledge at that stage in his career.

Although some officers subsequently attend the Defence Academy of the UK [Command and Staff Training] at Shrivenham, *'Training future commanders and staff officers of the UK and international armed services'* it is perhaps surprising the UKAFSJS does not feature in the syllabus, so his knowledge of Service law at that stage in his career would have been enhanced only by his experiences, if any, by taking hearings as a junior officer.

The charges against an accused, in most cases, originate from the CO's Unit. On arrest by the Service Police, authority to retain the accused in custody is sought from the CO and that same CO will conduct the summary hearing and prior thereto, and where circumstances so dictate, will also sanction an internal investigation into the case. It is not the officers' place to question how hearings are conducted as the rules are laid down in the MSL, or question whether it might arguably fall foul of *Findlay- v- United Kingdom* [*1997* ECHR 8, 24 EHRR 221, 22107 1993] that is, on grounds of independence and impartiality.

It is clear from the outset the CO is an interested party at every level in the proceedings. Under this situation, he becomes an investigator, prosecutor and finally, 'Judge'. This can raise a point of bias set out in *R v Sussex Justices, Ex-parte McCarthy* [*1997* ECHR 8, 24 EHRR 221, 22107 1993] a leading authority on impartiality and recusant Judges where such issues arise.

Should the CO have any reservations about a case, he can seek guidance from the SPA / Forces Legal Team, who in turn can only refer to the Act or the MSL as the definitive source but they can remind him that he has a number of options in how he deals with a case should he feel uncomfortable about it; he can dismiss the case or, where there is *prima facie* a case to answer, he can hand down a modest sanction; he can refer the case for hearing in the CM if he feels it serious enough; before any hearing he can remind the AAO that the accused can elect for trial in the CM; he can carry on regardless and on conviction remind the accused that he has an automatic right of appeal to the SAC; he can convict and sentence knowing that the case will be reviewed, as all summary convictions are [MSL Ch15, paras. 1-15-1 to 1-15-10] the purpose being to identify reasons to refer the conviction to the SAC.

Notwithstanding, it is in law generally unsatisfactory for a case about which there is some doubt, to be disposed of summarily on the basis that it will be, or could be, passed up the line for a review by, e.g., a higher authority.

There is other pressure to add to this; where a junior officer or senior NCO brings a disciplinary case, there may well be issues of a CO wanting to be seen to support his junior staff, and, understandable as this might be, it should be avoided but is a serious consideration and brings into focus some of the points raised in the arguments at 5[C] above, 'Kangaroo Courts'. This does put a CO in a very difficult position.

Persons who join the Forces as lawyers, will do so under a Specialist Entrant and Re-entrant [SERE] scheme, or for the Army an eight-week Professionally Qualified Officer [PQO] course. On graduating, they will be required to work advising on military law or as advocates in the CM, the SCC or the SACs. They will in addition be required to train officers in military law. One point arises; teaching / lecturing staff working in civilian institutions are usually required to have some kind of formal qualifications, such as a Certificate in Education [Cert Ed.] or a post-graduate certificate in Education [PGCE] and if this is not a prerequisite for the Service training, quality of the delivery of a syllabus could be questionable.

If one were to look at, albeit the somewhat remote possibility, of a qualified solicitor or barrister joining the Forces as an engineer or RAF aircrew officer, he would be ineligible for a role as an AAO at summary hearings. If he were able to so act it could be with interesting results as he would be operating under a system which would be totally alien to all his previous professional training and practice and thereby, possibly, attract his disapprobation. Indeed, he would very likely advise his 'client' to elect for trial in the CM.

There are no full-time courses in the forces specifically for law, but the subject is touched on during other courses which may cover a number of topics, and with the substantial work which comprises the Act and the MSL, the law element on such courses cannot extend to any more than a basic introduction to the SJS, when, as is usual, there are more important elements of the training courses to deal with.

Effectively, therefore, we have persons unqualified except by rank, conducting a quasi-judicial process. The punishments which can be handed include 28 days detention [90 with HA], suspended detention, forfeiture of seniority [officers only], reduction in rank, a fine of up to 28 days' pay, reprimand or severe reprimand, stoppage of leave, service compensation order of up to £1,000. [Annex A to chapter 13 MSL - Summary hearing sentencing and punishments]. And recording on the PNC.

6. THE SUMMARY PROCESSES COMPARED.

One must look at what research has discovered thus far and consider how each of them, and how collectively, they impact on the hypothesis. The main issues are:-

The accused at summary trial is not allowed legal representation. The Accused's Assisting Officer cannot be a lawyer. Some legal aid available. In civilian courts, the accused is at every stage permitted legal representation, even on minor cases and legal aid is available.

The rules of evidence do not apply. The hearing is not regarded as 'a court' so the CO is not bound by the rules of evidence. This may be a convenience but the process fits neatly into the category of 'tribunal' so UNUDHR should apply. In civilian courts, the rules of evidence are strictly applied.

The process is inquisitorial whereby the CO asks all the questions and there is no separate intervention by either party, nor can the AAO ask questions directly of the 'prosecution' witnesses, as all questions come from the CO. In civilian courts, the process is adversarial with separate representation from each side. Neither the CO nor any other person at the hearing is legally qualified, but in civilian courts all personnel are legally qualified.

The CO acts as Judge and decides on guilt or innocence and on sentence, whereas in the civilian process, the Bench decide after hearing all the evidence.

The CO hears criminal and disciplinary [non-criminal] cases; Magistrates hear criminal cases. [ignoring such things as licensing extensions for pubs etc and other minor issues].

The accused has to stand throughout the hearing, but in the Magistrates courts he does not; he is seated and has the facility to read and refer to any documents and confer with his lawyer.

A conviction on disciplinary and criminal charges can be recorded on the police national computer. This is 'under review' [JAGO May 2017] to take account of the various issues concerning the Serviceman's role and circumstances. In the civilian courts, only criminal convictions appear on the PNC.

Conviction rate at summary hearings is 95% [approximately] but at CM is around 50% [HH Blackett, Judge Advocate General, 30 May 2017 - interview].

Appeal to the Summary Appeal Court can take up to 2 weeks to organise. JAG Office [ibid] regard this as too long. If referred to the Crown Court for trial if the Magistrates decide they cannot hear a case, it is possible that a person can be on bail for many months waiting for a trial date.

There is no Forces' equivalent of the Rehabilitation of Offenders' Act 1974. However, the Act does apply to a serviceman's record once he has left the Forces. The Act does apply in the civilian process, where only 'relevant' previous convictions will apply and be made known to the court before sentence.

The punishments available to the CO depend on the offender's rank. In civilian courts, punishments apply to everybody regardless of status.

The issues as set out in the Findlay-v-UK case [Rant, 1.20; 9.04/6;9.29 - 'independent and impartial tribunal'] are still present in summary hearings. In civilian processes, no independence or impartiality issues arise as they are both independent and impartial.

The above illustrates clearly how the two systems of justice differ. All the pre-hearing assistance afforded the accused and for which the Service is to be complimented, does not make up for the, possibly flawed, process which the CO, or a person he nominates to take the hearing, is bound to follow.

7. KEY ISSUES - SERVICE SUMMARY JUSTICE.

What are the issues of having cases heard by unqualified persons? There are myriad problems. Firstly, the lawmakers in the UK deem it necessary to sit three Magistrates in the lower court, guided by a professional. The higher Crown courts are all Judges' courts, and the criminal cases they hear can, with some exceptions, be the same as can be dealt with summarily by a CO, except where they have to be referred to the SPA for CM procedure.

The reasons for the staffing of the courts are clear; justice must be seen to be done and those who administer it are legal professionals who ensure the fairness of the proceedings. In a number of the quotes and sections of The Act or the MSL or policy statements, the word 'fair' comes up repeatedly - the SJS overview, summary hearing, chapter 11 'Dealing with Evidence', the summary sentencing guide, the MAA complains procedure, Article 6 and the UNUDHR.

It is not adequate to have just read the appropriate text or statute. Convictions have to be 'safe'; lawyers - be it the Judge or Magistrate, defence or prosecution - must know how to ask a question and get a full answer; the defence must know how to protect their clients against themselves. [A lawyer's duty is to the 'court'; he must disregard specific instructions from his client if they conflict with that duty. [Denning, MR, Rondel and Worsley, 1969, 1AC 191]]. Also, the prosecution must know what points to pursue and those to drop.

It is also worth noting, as the auto / biographies of some eminent Judges [e.g., Christmas Humphreys QC [1978] J P Eddy, QC [1960] *et al* frequently point out that a defence counsel can, from his own mouth condemn his client by 'injudicious' questioning, and the CO is just as likely as any Judge to pick up on it, and a layman is more likely than an experienced counsel to commit that *fau pax* where he fails to appreciate, for example, what particular elements comprise the offence with which the accused is charged.

The Service summary process is inquisitorial [Chapter 211 MSL], and in countries where this system operates, it is always handled by a *Judge* who decides the scope and range of a hearing, searches for facts, listens to witnesses examines documents, orders evidence to be taken and then makes such further inquiries as he deems necessary. It is unreasonable to suppose that a layman [the CO] can exercise the same degree of expertise necessary to arrive at a reliable conclusion, but, effectively, this is what he is tasked to do and which apart from being an unfair burden on the CO, is also unfair on the accused.

The adversarial process is one where each party has responsibility for finding and presenting their evidence. The Judges or Magistrates do not investigate the facts [or the evidence] but he will be able to question what he sees as 'conflicts' in the evidence, inter alia, and it is up to the jury [if in the Crown court] to decide which side they believe.

The summary procedure as used in HM forces '... *is not a court and the rules of evidence do not apply ...*' [chapter 11 MSL]. Any law dictionary will show at least 50 entries for 'evidence', and it is difficult to comprehend how a CO can decide on the admissibility or otherwise of a bit of evidence, or the weight he should attach to it without having been introduced to that substantial element of the law and which in civil proceedings is so essential in the fair administration of justice.

The consequences for a person convicted by a Service summary court can be serious and extend into his career as a civilian on leaving the Forces, as it can, in some cases, mean the conviction being placed on the Police National Computer [PNC]. Such offences include misconduct towards a senior officer, using force against a sentry, damage to, or loss of, public or Service property, obstructing or failing to assist a Service policeman, resisting arrest, offences relating to Service custody and offences of negligently doing an act that results in a prisoner's escape, allowing escape or unlawful release of prisoners [etc.], absence without leave [Reserve Forces Act 1996]. Quite why these should appear on the PNC is difficult to comprehend. Criminal convictions include a whole series of offences under the Theft Act, Misuse of Drugs Act, Criminal Damage Act, Criminal Attempts Act, Road Traffic Acts.

Kelly [2014] adds that having a criminal record does not assist in resettlement. The document makes interesting reading for anybody involved with the Armed Forces, and which will inevitably include their return to civilian life, and a criminal record could be just one more obstacle they might have to deal with.

Consider another fairness aspect of the summary process; the MSL at chapter 13 Annex B lists *'Punishments which may be awarded to each rank or rate'* and lists the ranks from Officer, Warrant Officer, Senior non-commissioned officers, corporals, leading / lance corporals and able rates / marines / soldiers and airmen. This is discriminatory. Article 7 of the United Nations Universal Declaration of Human Rights [UNUDHR], drafted by the United nations Commission on Human Rights in December 1948 states ...

> *'...We are all equal before the law and are entitled without*

any discrimination to equal protection of the law.' Thus, everyone must be treated equally regardless of race, gender, national origin, colour, ethnicity, religion, disability or other characteristics without privilege, discrimination or bias ...'.

That this applies to *rank* is beyond question. Punishments cover forfeiture of seniority [Officers only] then fines, severe reprimand, reprimand, admonition, Service compensation order, Reduction in rank [not officers] Stoppage of leave, detention, payment orders [Able rates etc. only] and restriction of privileges [Able etc. rates only].

There must be reasoning behind this provision, but it appears to fly in the face of the equality principle. It may be 'unseemly' to have an officer committed to a term in the military corrective centre at Colchester, but where otherwise a spell in detention is an option in sentencing other ranks, then it is only reasonable to apply it to all ranks, and as far as an officer is concerned, he would in all probability choose to resign his commission on his being released, but, unless part of his punishment, he should not be forced to resign.

Ignoring an accused's individual problems and circumstances such as should be accounted for in any summary, or indeed in any, court hearing, can only result in seriously adverse effects on the morale of serviceman and deter recruiting. Otherwise, and rightly or wrongly, the impression is that the system is established for the convenience of the Service.

Morgan [2008] points out that most civilian systems have also developed pre-court or administrative criminal justice decision-making whereby some criminal matters are, or can be, dealt with by the police and/or the prosecuting authorities without their coming before the courts at all. He adds that ...

...the offences dealt with in this manner tend to be the most common and straightforward, for which the penalty is normally pecuniary, making good the deficiency or the harm done, or involving the issue of a recorded warning. This differential approach is judged proportionate to the gravity of the offences and the risks of injustice involved. Each

decision-making tier has its own safeguards'.

Prosper Mwedzi [2014] acknowledges that the Military Justice System *'exhibits some striking parallels to the civilian justice system'* but he does not comment on the value or fairness of the Services summary justice process. Where the barristers and solicitors involved in the CM cases may have been of some benefit in the pursuit of fairness in disciplinary and criminal cases, as they are disqualified from participating in Service summary hearings, who holds the brief on fairness in those proceedings?
What Mwedzi did mention was Findlay v The United Kingdom [110/1995/616/706] 25 February 1997: *independence and impartiality of court-martial; convening officer central to prosecution and closely linked to prosecuting authorities]* and bearing in mind the outcome of this case, any comparison with the summary hearings will show it to be even less 'independent and impartial' than in the CM.

The same comments on the CM were made by Gates [2008] who, regrettably, ignores the summary process.

A conviction can have long-lasting effects on the individual whilst he is serving, as there is no Forces equivalent of the Rehabilitation of Offenders' Act 1974, so convictions are never 'spent' or removed from a service record, so old, and perhaps minor offences, will always be a consideration on promotion or by commissioning boards and although it can be argued that the board would [or perhaps should] ignore old convictions or disciplinary actions, would they? It is difficult to imagine that they would not be swayed against a candidate who might in all other respects be an ideal choice for promotion or commissioning.

The offences will still be on his service record once discharged into civilian life after a full career in HM forces, and may become an issue were he to unfortunately later engage with the Criminal Justice System.

It may be that the civilian population was in many cases also treated harshly by the criminal justice system or certainly by today's standards, but there arise a number of important factors which are due consideration when comparing the justice systems. Firstly, all criminals who face justice are now treated according to the civil law; secondly, the armed forces are working in the service of their country and should be treated at least as fairly as the civilian population and finally, why is there still not one process which applies to every person regardless of occupation and rank? Any factors which may apply to the work the serviceman is doing, the stress he might be under or other notable factors can be the subject of a mitigation plea in the case of a finding of guilt.

If the Service is determined to remain with the *status quo* of the summary justice system where it is seen to be unfair in its application, and if it does not acknowledge any obvious fault-lines, then those who make policy decisions and who have the power to make change cannot be surprised if they find themselves in collision with the ECtHR and, ultimately, with the civil UK courts.

8. CONCLUSION AND RECOMMENDATIONS.

[A] Conclusion

The introduction to this dissertation stated that the Services operate a form of criminal summary justice which does not easily identify with the civil system. We have seen in the intervening pages that this assertion appears to be well founded. What has not been shown is any justification the Services have for pursuing their particular form of summary justice. The overriding considerations are that the CO is unqualified and yet has to apply a judicial process. This was never going to work and where it had been applied in the distant past there was very probably no alternative process.

One has to consider why this summary process continues. It is certainly convenient, in that there are no legal professionals involved in the hearings, so there is an obvious cost saving. Secondly, as there would be no legal arguments on either side, there would be a time saving. The summary hearings are not 'courts' so there was no need to account for the usual protocols as to the hearing of evidence. Nor is there any need to look beyond the two main volumes, being The Act and the MSL, which effectively encompass all the information the participants need to conduct summary hearings as they are by The Act authorised to do. Neither the AAO nor the CO is therefore going to wade through Rumbold's *Automatism as Defence in Criminal Law* or Joyce's *Criminology and Criminal Justice.*

Consider a few of the main issues;

The lack of adherence to the rules of evidence;
The CO will see the accused's service record before the hearing;
The prohibition of lawyers representing the accused;
A single entity representing all the court 'officials';
The lack of independence and impartiality [Article 6];
The inquisitorial procedure.

How this can be a fair representation of the UNUDHR on fairness in tribunals does take some explaining.

As regards disciplinary offences, it appears that, too, needs some overhaul as the questions of impartiality and independence arise in a process which puts those hearing a case in a difficult position. The Commanding Officers and the junior officers can find themselves having to support their junior staff in a case where the officer hearing or reviewing the case considers it not proved. Bear in mind that these cases differ from a criminal action as there is unlikely to be any material trail but rely on principally witness statements which can in certain instances be as helpful to one side as to the other. The relationship therefore between the perhaps over-zealous, possibly a charitable description, NCO and the CO who acts fairly and according to the evidence could become strained and difficult. However, 'twas ever thus, but it does raise the issue of whether the two parties could ever be so far removed from each other, operationally speaking, so as to obviate this major problem.

Added to that, is an Army trooper or an RAF airman going to stand before the CO and contradict the evidence of his sergeant or corporal, or even junior officer, who might have brought the charge or that of other NCOs and officers who will appear for the 'prosecution'? It is a point of considerable gravity but is likely to be less of an issue if the proceedings were out of the confines of a CO's or NCO's office, and conducted in a proper, legal forum.

The same will almost certainly apply to a case of a MAAs, where the reviewing officer might share an office with the NCOs who initiate the action, and notwithstanding that the same NCOs may not themselves be overly familiar with the correct procedures in bringing the MAA.

Regrettably, this can taint the process with some of the points raised in the *kangaroo courts'* charge at 5[C] above. It is not unknown for there to be group punishments or for the reviewing officer to be not only dismissive of a review, but downright offensive to the offenders; certainly not his role. [The researcher has evidence of this on file as with the comments on the DVD but can only release it on a basis of strict confidentiality].

Currently the SJS comprises the following;

Commanding Officers' summary hearings for criminal cases;
Commanding Officers' summary hearings for disciplinary cases;
Summary Cases Review;
Summary Appeal Court;
Courts Martial [criminal and disciplinary cases];
Court Martial Appeal Court;
Service Civilian Court;
Minor Administrative Actions;
Major Administrative Actions;

The Courts Martial element of the Service Justice system is a substantial organisation staffed by law professionals, but why should it be limited to hearing only criminal cases not dealt with at summary stage? We have seen that the summary tribunals [by definition that it what they are] follow a process which would not be recognised by any civil legal practitioner.

Although it may not in the past have been practical to engage a formal criminal and disciplinary process but rather one of convenience when dealing with cases arising on active service, using the COs' authority and the use of Field and General Courts Martial, the options and facilities available today make it eminently possible to operate a far better system of justice which matches at least that of the civil process. Remember Jepson ...

> '...despite the Services' unique role [the application of lethal force on behalf of the nation] and its potentially expeditionary nature, the SJS ... should be both independent and professional...'

... and the MOD Service Prosecuting Authority website ...

> '...it remains the intention that Service law should reflect the provisions of the civilian justice system as far as it is sensible and practical to do so. This involves recognition of the need to sustain Service ethos and discipline. Attention to detail in preserving the best and changing those procedures which do not serve us well, will be another target of our attention in the years ahead ...'.

The CO is authorised by The Act to carry out his function at summary, criminal hearings, but should he be prohibited from so doing? The last word on this is from the Judge Advocate General [JAG] HH Jeff Blackett, the senior Judge in the Armed Forces justice system, who stated that ...

> '... the time when the criminal law could be easily assimilated and applied with a dash of common sense by unqualified people, even if of outstanding intelligence, has long passed'. [Rant 'The Court Martial and Service Law' at 1.09 p.4 [3rd edition Oxford University Press 08/2009].

What also makes this a pressing issue is that criminal convictions, which may not - for a number of reasons - have been fairly achieved, are recorded on the PNC; however, the JAG pointed out that this was 'under review' [Interview, 30 May 2017]. In the meantime, however, it still reflects adversely on Service leavers.

A CO's role in summary hearings must come under scrutiny, and at the very least addressed in the forthcoming Review [due

2021] or it is possible there will be further applications to the ECHR then the ECtHR making an appropriate Order. Bearing in mind that the Rant comment was made in 2009, it will be surprising if the reviewing panel have not already taken this on board, and will make appropriate changes.

So, why were procedural errors highlighted by the European Court of Human Rights [ECtHR] and corrected in the CM process, not applied to the summary process in the 2016 review? The full answer is ...

> '...The Service Justice System is kept under regular review and .. is subject to parliamentary scrutiny every 5 years when the Armed Forces Act 2006 is renewed. The last such renewal was in 2016 during the passage of the Armed Forces Act. As the Act progressed through Parliament, key aspects of the system were scrutinised and debated and no significant changes to the system were made. However, the provisions of the Armed Forces Act 2006 will next need to be renewed by 2021 and we are already beginning to think about how best to use that opportunity to ensure our Service Justice System continues to meet the needs of our Armed Forces ...' [MOD UK, email, 06 July 2017]

Change must be enacted, and justice done, by re-jigging the various departments of the SPA, the MCS *et al* and undertaking revision of The Act and the MSL regardless of cost.

Considering now the application of different punishments according to rank, this may well be an historical issue, but makes a mockery of the equality principle. In the civil process, the same punishments apply to whomsoever is convicted. The only difference might be where an offender could receive a more severe punishment if guilty of a 'breach of trust' or 'should have known better', which is usually applied to the more intelligent offender, but no punishments are reserved specifically for certain classes of person, intelligent or otherwise. Although this may be a contentious issue, the same rules should apply in Service courts, irrespective of the rank of the offender. The UNUDHR again ...

'... Everyone is entitled in full equality to a fair and public hearing by an independent and impartial tribunal, in the determination of his rights and obligations and of any criminal charge against him.'

Referring to the SPA and to the JAG quotes above, and to the issues with the *status quo*, there is no good reason for perpetuating a system of summary justice which the Service authorities themselves appear be keen to review. The reasons set out in this dissertation must add to the determination of the MOD to grasp the opportunity which presents itself with the forthcoming review, and if it is to be effected by 2021, the draftsmen, lawyers, the MOD and Parliament should now be at work to bring about the essential reforms.

[B] Recommendations.

It is hoped that the Reviewers consider these recommendations in undertaking the 2021Review. The Board may already be looking at a substantial redrafting of The Act and the MSL if it is to account for the changes necessary to ensure that our Servicemen face a fairer hearing when involved in the Service summary criminal or disciplinary processes.

It will not be beyond the resources of the SPA and the MCS et al to establish summary processes which fall in line with those of the civil courts. The Defence Service Prosecuting Authority' website *states ...*

'...It remains the intention that Service law should reflect the provisions of the civilian justice system as far as it is sensible and practical to do so...' A reminder.

The recommendations are as follows;

1. The power of Commanding Officers to hear criminal cases be abolished.

2. That all relevant authorities establish a Service Summary Court [SSC] with a Judge Advocate [qualified barrister or solicitor] to preside. To be run along similar lines to the Magistrates' Courts to

deal with all criminal cases at first instance with the same provisions with regard to election for trial in the CM and appeal to the SAC.

3. The accused be permitted to have legal representation or otherwise he can act IP; McKenzie friend can attend if the accused so wishes.

4. If on overseas duties personnel be subject as currently to the Status of Forces Agreements or any Memoranda of Understanding where appropriate.

5. No SSC or CM convictions to be recorded on the PNC.

6. Convictions [criminal and disciplinary] will be cleared [or not disclosed] after a period to be determined by the relevant authorities in consultation with other interested parties.

7. That Commanding Officers only deal with serious disciplinary cases which can, on election, be referred to the CM or on appeal by the offender as now. Less serious cases to be dealt with by the MAA process, suitably expanded to deal not only with 'personal failings' but also minor disciplinary offences; seriousness of disciplinary offences to be categorised by available punishments. Cases dealt with under the new MAA process must be carefully monitored to ensure it is not exploited, is used strictly in accordance with the laid-down procedures and that the MAA reviewing officer is an officer from another unit [either within the same station or from another station] and the subject of the MAA be fully apprised of his right to refer the case upwards via the Service Complaints procedure.

8. Service records only to be scrutinised after conviction.

9. The major administrative action be abolished [as it will become a duplication].

10. The Service Civilian Courts [SCC] be abolished and all civilian contractors agree as a term of their engagement to be subject to the SSC as above for criminal offences and the MAA as above for

disciplinary matters;

11. That the DVD '*Information for the accused*' be substantially revised and that Service recruits receive more instruction on Service law than just viewing the DVD;

12. That the distinction of punishments and rank be abolished.

ANNEXES

Annex A - Judge Advocate General's Office   - Response to Questionnaire

Annex B - Military Court Service - Response to Questionnaire

Annex C - MAA etc information

Annex A

JAG's Office

Response to Questionnaire

Respondent : Judge Advocate General's Office.

Date of meeting; 30 May 2017

Location: Military Court Centre, Bulford, Wiltshire.

Date of JAG responding to researcher's notes: 08 June 2017

---

1. Does a CO or other authorised Officer have power to refer a finding of guilt after hearing to HA just for sentencing;

No; if the case is one which the CO feels he does not have the power to deal with he will refer it to the SPA.

2. Can the 'prosecution' [complainant] appeal a CO's decision to dismiss a case or appeal against sentence if they consider it to be too lenient;

No.

3. Can a CO during a hearing adjourn proceedings and then for whatever reason have it dealt with by CM;

If the CO realised that something more serious had occurred than was before him, he could stop proceedings and refer the case to the Service Police for further investigation.

4. If yes, does this have to be at the request of or with the consent of the accused;

No.

5. Can a summary hearing proceed without the accused being present should the accused choose not to be present at the hearing;

No; the accused can be ordered to attend, and if he / she does not do so another offence would arise and it is possible that under those circumstances it would be referred to a CM.

6. Whereas the accused cannot have a lawyer as his AAO can he have a
non-service i.e., a civilian non-lawyer as his AAO;

No.

7. Does the accused / AAO receive all written evidence and all documents [e.g., previous / service record sheet] before hearing;

Yes; until all those documents are made available by the CO the case will not be heard.

8. Does the accused / AAO receive copies of all written evidence and all other documents after hearing to help with any decision to appeal to the SAC;

The defendant has 14 days to decide if he wishes to apply to the SAC and is entitled to legal advice to assist him in making the decision; the decision will be based on [probably] not so much the evidence, but as to whether he feels that the conviction or the sentence was unfair; e.g., that he did not actually commit the offence or if otherwise, that the punishment was harsh. In any event, a CO only has the power to hand down 28 days detention [without HA] but up to 90 days with HA.

This right to appeal to the SAC is regarded as a major safeguard against miscarriages of justice by the summary process and all cases are reviewed by the Reviewing

Authority which can refer the matter to the SAC if they find an irregularity. However, there may be a reluctance to appeal as the process can take weeks to organise, and with no certain outcome, it is believed that the offender would rather just 'take it on the chin'.

Would this put off the genuinely innocent person ?

With a conviction rate of about 95% for summary hearings and about 50% for CM, that might be some little comfort. However, if all the accused persons were to apply for trial in the CM on this basis, the CM system would be grossly overburdened. Hence, alternatives should be available to deal with this possibility.
In addition, all summary convictions are reviewed by a Reviewing Officer [RO] appointed by the Defence Council [section 152 of the Act] for finding or punishment the purpose of which is to identify any reasons for referring the finding, sentence [or activation of a suspended sentence] to the SAC. [Ch 15 MSL]. The RO is not 'legally' qualified and has no judicial function and cannot therefore determine errors of law during the summary hearing but they can identify errors and then refer them to the SAC for resolution.

This policy is to identify disciplinary trends and issues and to assist in the achievement of a common approach to summary findings and punishments within the Services as a whole.

9.   Is the order of evidence as per or very similar to those of the civilian Magistrates' courts [MCR 1981 s. 13] - or is there no guidance on this;

No; the MCR do not apply at summary hearings. However, the principles 'ensure best practice and fairness to the accused'. One has to assume that the principles referred to are those set out as guidelines for the CO in dealing with summary hearings. These are set out fully in the MSL at Chapter 11 [11 pages of guidance] based on the MCR.

10.   Who else, if anybody, can be present at the hearings [e.g.;

family or a kind of 'next-friend'];

Nobody;

11. Is the accused able to be seated during hearings – or does he have to stand;

The accused must stand.

12. Does the CO have absolute control during the hearing ? In the DVD the Regimental Sergeant Major [RSM] ' *runs the hearing on behalf of the CO' and helps the proceedings go smoothly'* Please explain;

The CO has overall control. This aspect of the DVD presentation, inter alia, is one discussed in the Dissertation which deal specifically with the DVD.

13. Does the CO have assistance during the process – e.g., the equivalent of a justices' clerk and is that the role of the adjutant [refer the DVD];

The staff present during the hearing are there for the reasons as set out in the DVD, and the adjutant is not required to take verbatim notes. Should the matter go to appeal, all the evidence will be heard again - the SAC is a 'de novo' hearing; i.e., based on an order directing a new trial after a mis-trial involving an irregularity with the first trial being regarded as a nullity However, although the Judge will have seen some of the papers, SPA will produce a new bundle. The SAC procedure is based on that of an appeal from the Magistrates to the Crown Court.

14. Is a verbatim record of the hearing prepared so as to be available in case of an appeal and if so by whom;

No. See above.

15. Is there any medical examination of the accused before hearings e.g. to establish *inter alia* mental capacity;

No; unless there are concerns [which the CO might have where the symptoms are obvious] as to an accused's mental or physical state, or unless the accused / the AAO requests it for some reason. The same applies in any civilian court, e.g., where the defendant collapses in the dock.

16. What provisions are made for any accused who may be regarded as being 'vulnerable' - considering inter alia, age;

There is a system for the Armed Forces; vulnerable personnel would not get through training and would be weeded out at initial training.

The CO or the AAO should be aware of any circumstances such as this and all necessary allowances should be made. If there are any questions re this, then it would be reflected in conviction [if the CO proceeded] or he would take advice before any proceedings.

Bearing in mind the information in the part of this dissertation entitled 'Who are we dealing with' it might be appropriate for a 'vulnerable' person to have a kind of 'next friend' [though not in the strict legal sense] to attend the hearing with the accused or indeed to be with him throughout the whole process. This situation should not ever occur.

17. Can the accused / AAO request a medical / psychiatric examination prior to a hearing where there may be issues where an accused could be regarded as unable to fully appreciate his situation [not talking about McNaughton of course];

The above answers apply. In the unlikely case of insanity then there would be no trial and other provisions would apply.

18. [a] What is the extent of a CO's training for hearing cases summarily; and [b] where the CO delegates his authority to a junior officer, is that subject to that officer having has suitable training;

It is understood that officers who are chosen for Command posts will have been given at least one day's training; as regards his handing over to his junior officers, it is not known if they must, as a condition precedent, have also received some training. In Rant on The Court Martial and Service Law [3rd edition. HHJ Jeff Blackett] there is mention of the MOD overstating the training given to some service personnel but that applied to the training of Board members at the Court Martial following the case of Morris - v - UK [2002 34 EHRR 1253; Rant etc. at 5.80 & 5.81]; those who advise the COs have more training.

The researcher has applied to the RAF College Cranwell [Officer Cadet Training establishment] and to the Director Legal Services, High Wycombe, for information on the training aspect, but has to date received no response from either of them.

19. Who determines the syllabus for preparing officers for command posts course content and is it drafted by lawyers;

Refer above;

20. Who delivers the training e.g.; are they professional lecturers and / or lawyers;

Refer above;

21. Is there any CPD / mentoring or equivalent after initial training [as with Magistrates];

Refer above;

22. Do the provisions of the Rehabilitation of Offenders' Act 1974 [or any equivalent] apply to summary offences or to CM offences;

No. The offences remain on the Service Record for life. However, the older they are the less relevant. There are many cases of service personnel who have been punished and even sent to detention early in their careers who nevertheless

become senior NCOs or officers.

So old [not defined] offences would 'probably' not influence a promotion / commissioning board. But then again, it would be hard to imagine that no account would be taken of them if, all other things being equal, candidates A and B were 'neck and neck' at the finishing line.

23. If not, for how long does the offence 'count' on an offender's record;

Refer above;

24. When – if at all and apart from death – will a serviceman's record be 'clean';

Not even on death; Servicemen's records are available to public and family long after his death.

25. Apart from offences which are on the PNC do the civilian authorities have access to a serviceman's record during [a] his period in the Service and [b] on his returning to civilian life;

No unless the serviceman wishes to disclose. However, the issue of posting a service offence on the PNC is somewhat contentious and it is expected that this policy will be reviewed not least because the circumstances under which members of the armed forces operate may have some bearing on the accused's mental and physical demeanour at the time the offence was committed, and it is perhaps unfair to apply the same rules as would apply to civilians.

26. What is the thinking behind having different punishments and scales available for different ranks e.g., Officers, NCOs and other ranks;

This is historical and requires further research; it will not be pursued in this paper. However, there are many distinctions between officers and other ranks all of which have a bearing; in some cases, officers are dealt with more harshly.

27. Does the CO have access to an accused's service record before any hearing;

Yes;

28. With HA and if an accused opts for summary trial can the CO deal with the case and if found guilty can sentence be decided by the JAG's office or must the CO stick to his powers of sentence;

Yes, he must.

29. Are there any formal committal hearings by the CO [to assess the evidence and seriousness of the case] to determine whether it is a CM case;

There are two parts to this; first the accused has an unfettered right to elect trial in the CM however minor the offence. He is entitled to legal advice to help him make that decision. If the case becomes before the CO [i.e., not directly to the SPA] he may decide to refer it to the SPA for trial in the CM because of its seriousness or if it is complicated. However, the CO may have a formal hearing to help him determine that.

30. Is the AAO able to seek advice from the Service Legal Team [as the CO can on certain matters];

The accused and the AAO can take legal advice - either free or from the firms of solicitors who deal with service issues. Legal aided is also available via the Armed Forces Criminal Legal Aid Authority, part of the Military Court Service. He is entitled to legal advice as to whether to apply for CM trial and afterwards to decide on whether to appeal to the SAC.

31. The Rules of Evidence 'do not apply' ; how does the MCS reconcile this with having to apply them to documentary evidence in case of an application to the SAC [or review];

This issue is fully explained in the text above

32. How long does it take [on average] to convene a Court Martial once the JAG's office has been notified of an impending action;

This depends on the seriousness of the case; if this is an election by the accused for trial in the CM it will be referred to the SPA and will be dealt with as any other trial. Clearly, election trials should be easier to process but the JAG's office suggests that they still take too long to be listed.

Investigation / Civilian / MP

1. Do the MP assume any powers over the accused that are not afforded the civilian force;

Not discussed; but JAG's comments as follows; The Services are bound by the PACE codes of conduct and carry out investigations in the same way. The only additional power they have is that they can give a lawful, order to an accused to attend for questioning but they cannot force him to answer questions etc.

2. Is there any formal cautioning of an accused by the MP before questioning;

Not discussed; but JAG's comments as follows; yes; identical to the civilian force.

3. Are interviews taped;

Not discussed; but JAG's comments as follows; yes; identical to the civilian force.

4. Is the AAO or next friend [with minors] or lawyers permitted to be present during all interviews;

Not discussed; but JAG's comments as follows; yes; identical to the civilian force. Accused has a right to a lawyer from the

start and if he does want one, he gets one.

5. Do the MP have access to the accused's service record before any charges are preferred;

Not discussed; but JAG's comments as follows; no unless relevant to the investigation.

6. Do the MP operate any 'bail' provisions and if so who can apply and what conditions can be set if any;

Not discussed; but JAG's comments as follows; Service police have some powers of arrest during interviews as the civilian police; If a civilian is to be held in custody he must be brought before a Judge Advocate for a custody hearing - same as a bail hearing. The Judge Advocate may order custody for up to seven days to be reviewed every seven days thereafter and with the accused's consent, after he has taken legal advice, extended to 28 days. The Judge Advocate may release with conditions

7. Do the MP have access to the PNC for an accused for offences committed prior to his joining the Service;

Not discussed; but JAG's comments as follows; Yes.

ANNEX B

Military Court Service

Response to Questionnaire

Respondent : Miles Rowley, Deputy Director MCS

Date of meeting; 28 June 2017

Location: Military Court Services; Upavon,
Wiltshire,

Date of DDMCS responding to researcher's notes:
04 July 2017

---

1. Is the MCS / SPA / DLS responsible for the DVD aid for those accused of a summary offence ? have you seen it ?

The MCS was not directly involved in the production of the DVD, although some of it was filmed at the Military Court Centres. As I recall, Army Legal Services were the principal consultants from an editorial perspective.

2. With summary convictions rate 95% and CM 50%, with proper advice the accused might be wise to opt for CM; if they were to, the CM system would be grossly overburdened [JAG's office 30 May 2017]; what alternatives are or could be made available to deal with this possibility?

One alternative previously floated by the JAG was

for the Judges to sit as Magistrates (without boards) to deal with summary business, although the presumed entitlement on the part of the defendant to legal representation would attract a cost. Worth checking with the JAG whether he still considers this a viable proposition.

3.   The time to arrange a CM depends on the seriousness of the case; where there is an election by the accused for trial in the CM it will be referred to the SPA to be dealt with as any other trial. However, the JAG's 's office suggests that cases take too long to be listed.

SPA: 'No prosecution authority can predict the level of crime or the volume of cases which will be referred to it in a given year. In the case of the SPA there are clearly risks in terms of case-flow. It is conceivable that the changes made by the Act [Armed Forces Act 2006] may see a reduction in summary dealing, and a higher volume of cases being referred to the SPA. Where COs follow proper procedure, are alert to their responsibilities, and are able to instil trust in those under command, summary dealing, or minor administrative action can still be both an effective and appropriate manner of dealing with less serious criminal or disciplinary offences. Reducing delay is a key aim of the Service Justice System. It remains the intention that Service law should reflect the provisions of the civilian justice system as far as it is sensible and practical to do so. This involves recognition of the need to sustain Service ethos and discipline. Attention to detail in preserving the best and changing those procedures which do not serve us well, will be another target of our attention in the years ahead.'

4. As we know, justice delayed is justice denied. What proposals has the MCS made to the SPA / MOD to reduce the time taken to arrange CMs ?

The MCS, in conjunction with the judiciary and SPA, has worked in recent months on the implementation of the Better Case Management policy – based on the system introduced in the civilian criminal justice system in the past 2/3 years; principal aims/objectives include a reduction in both resources and time taken in bringing cases to the court martial. A Practice Memorandum covering the detail should be available from the JAG's office.

5. What percentage [approximately] of cases heard in the CM are criminal ?

A rough calculation based on 2016 data suggests a split in the region of 68% criminal and 32% disciplinary offences.

6. Who is responsible for initiating change within the SJS ?

Governance and policy development within the Service Justice System is the responsibility of the Service Justice Board and Service Justice Executive Group. Details available from Caron Tassel at MOD.

7. What input / influence if any does the MCS have in training of Officers who may take up Command roles and dispense summary justice ?

None. Our input/influence is limited to proceedings in the courts.

ANNEX C

The Queen's Regulations for the Royal Air Force

Fifth Edition 1999 inc. Amendment List No 36

[S. 1027 - Re; Administrative Action [AA]

Administrative Action. Sponsor: ACOS Pers Pol (RAF) (1) The RAF system of administrative action encompasses a range of processes employed to rehabilitate, censure or initiate administrative sanctions in respect of an individual for professional or personal failings. It is separate from disciplinary action under the Air Force Act although it may be appropriate to initiate administrative action as a consequence of, and in addition to, civil proceedings or military disciplinary action. Reports under this paragraph are not to be regarded as a substitute for disciplinary action. The process for administrative action is described in AP 3392, Vol 5, Leaflet 127. It is a graduated 2-stage process and comprises:

a. Minor Administrative Action

(1) Report Back Muster/Parades
(2) Extra Duties/Tasks
(3) Extra Work
(4) Informal/Formal Interviews
(5) Return to Unit (RTU)

b. Major Administrative Action

(1) Formal Warning

The specific procedures for Minor Administrative Action, formal warnings and Administrative Reports (ARs) are dealt with in Air Publication (AP) 3392, Vol 5, Leaflets 128, 129 and 130 respectively. These procedures apply to all non-commissioned ranks and officers.

(2) Administrative Report (AR)

It is not necessary to exhaust each stage of administrative action before initiating the next level if the seriousness of the case warrants the immediate use of a higher level of sanction. If a CO or commander of a group or command or other reporting officer considers that an AR is appropriate in relation to an officer, warrant officer, non-commissioned officer or airman serving under his command, a report is to be raised in accordance with para 1b(2) of this QR immediately it is warranted, following the guidance in AP 3392, Vol 5 Leaflet 130.

(3) The individual reported on is to have a copy of the original report disclosed to them for their signature and be advised of their right of reply. The individual is to be informed of the procedures for the disposal of the report given in AP 3392, Vol 5 Leaflet 130. In all cases, all personnel involved in the case, including the subject of the report, are to be reminded of the document handling caveat in relation to third parties. In cases of a sexual nature, given the sensitive information likely to be contained in such reports, extra care should be taken in the staffing process, particularly in relation to disclosure Chap 15 DISCIPLINE QR(RAF) 15-14 AL32/June 13

(4) The initiating officer may recommend one or more specific sanctions in an AR; the sanctions

available for officers and airmen are detailed below. If, during the course of preparing the AR, a lesser form of administrative action is considered more appropriate the Report may be withdrawn and a Formal Interview or a Formal Warning initiated instead. However, where a more severe sanction is recommended, the case is to be re-disclosed to the subject.

(5) In all cases (except those based upon the subject having been given a custodial sentence) where it is considered appropriate to terminate an officer's commission (including compulsory retirement and being called upon to retire) or compulsorily discharge of an airman from the Service, no disposal decision shall be made until the individual has been given an opportunity to make representations in person to the appropriate disposal authority. During such an interview, the subject has the right to be accompanied by a Service Colleague in accordance with AP 3392, Vol. 5, Leaflet 130. For the avoidance of doubt, the right to an interview under this QR does not extend to individuals who are serving a custodial term.

Sanctions

(6) Airmen. In addition to the ability of the chain of command to initiate Minor Administrative Action and/or Formal Warnings, reports by COs on airmen under this regulation may be raised in relation to one of the following courses of action, for consideration by the appropriate disposal authority:

(a) Discharge from the Service under the terms of para 607(6)(b) or (c), 607(7)(b) or (c), 607(18), 607(21) or 607(22)(b) or 607(24)(b) or 607(25) (a) or (b) as appropriate.

(b) Reduction in rank:

(i) An airman who is reduced in substantive rank but not discharged is, except where over-riding Service reasons apply, to be posted.

(ii) The reduction of an airman is to take effect immediately the order is signed. If, as a consequence of the reduction, the airman is to be re-mustered, and he opts for discharge under para 607(10)(e) in the circumstances at sub-paragraph (c), he is to be discharged in his existing trade in the rank to which he has been reduced.

(iii) A Warrant Officer or NCO is not to be reduced below the highest aircraftman rank appropriate to his trade career plan, or the highest aircraftman rank to which he is qualified unless reduction is ordered by the appropriate authority because of an offence against trade practices, or on the basis of general inefficiency as a tradesman. See also paras 623A, 1118 and 1061(20) or (21).

(iv) An airman (including an airman transferred from other arms of HM Forces) may not be reduced to a rank actually or relatively lower than the rank in which he initially enlisted, re-enlisted or re-entered the RAF. Cases where reduction below this rank appears to be warranted are to be referred to the HQ AIR, APC for advice.

(v) Where appropriate, a direction which includes a reduction in rank is also to state the date on which restoration of rank is to be considered by a Board of Officers at ACOS Manning. (See AP 3392 Volume 2 Leaflet 570).

(c) Re-mustering. Reduction in rank to a rank inappropriate to the airman's trade or career pattern may result in consequential re-mustering. Similarly, compulsory re-mustering may result in consequential reduction in rank. However, when an airman is recommended for re-mustering and consequential reduction in rank is not considered justified, re-mustering in existing rank may be recommended. An airman who is to be compulsorily or consequentially re-mustered is to attend the Trade Reselection Centre (TRC) at ACOS Manning, for consideration of suitability for and availability of training. Where the individual is not considered suitable or no suitable training vacancy is available the individual will be discharged. The airman will also be given the option of discharge under QR 607(10)(e). An airman who is to be compulsorily re-mustered and consequentially reduced in rank who accepts an alternative trade is to be reduced to the rank of Leading Aircraftman or woman if they have completed 6 months service or reduced to the rank of Aircraftman or woman if they have completed less than 6 months service.

Chap 15 DISCIPLINE QR(RAF) 15-15 AL32/Jun 13

In both cases, they should be re-mustered in their existing trade under training in the new trade from the date of commencement of formal training.

(d) Posting. An airman may be posted to another unit or area where it is considered desirable in the interest of the Service. Such posting will usually but not exclusively be associated with another administrative sanction.

(e) Retention. There are cases where the raising of an AR under this regulation is mandatory and would normally lead to the airman being discharged.

However, if exceptional circumstances exist and it is in the Service Interest, a Unit may raise an AR with a recommendation that the individual be retained.

(7) Non-Commissioned Aircrew – Reduction or Re-mustering. In addition to para (6) above, it is to be borne in mind that fully trained non-commissioned aircrew cannot be employed productively if reduced below the rank of sergeant. A decision to reduce a non-commissioned aircrew below this rank will involve either re-mustering and reduction to the rank of aircraftman (or any higher rank up to junior technician which had previously been held) or discharge.

(8) Officers. In addition to the ability of the chain of command to initiate Minor Administrative Action and/or Formal Warnings, reports by COs on officers under this regulation may recommend the following course of action:

(a) Terminate an officer's commission, including being called upon to retire, relinquish or resign his commission or be transferred to the reserve, or be compulsorily retired or transferred to the reserve iaw para 2905.

(b) Removed from branch. An officer who is removed from their branch will be considered for employment in another branch.
(c) Delay time promotion.

(d) Removal of Acting Rank.

(e) An officer may be posted to another appointment commensurate to their training, ability and experience. Such posting will usually but not exclusively be associated with another administrative sanction.

(f) Interview with AOC, in association with Formal Warning.

(9) When under a Suspended Sentence of Service Detention and the individual commits a subsequent offence, in addition to considering formal disciplinary action and the activation of the suspended sentence, admin action should also be considered.

List of Abbreviations

AAO - Accused's Assisting Officer

ACOS - Assistant Chief of [Air] Staff

AFA   - Armed Forces Act 2006

AFDA - Armed Forces Discipline Act 2000

AFMSPS - Armed Forces Monthly Service Personnel Statistics

AGAI - Army General Administrative Instruction 67

APC - Not listed in Abbreviations and Acronyms for the RAF

BAFF - British Armed Forces Federation

CJS - Criminal Justice System

CLMT - Command Leadership Management Training

CO - Commanding Officer

CM - Court Martial

CODO - Contractors on Deployed Operations

CPD - Continuing Professional Development

CPS - Crown Prosecution Service

DC - Defence Council

DLS - Directorate of Legal Services

DSC - Defence Select Committee

DSP - Director of Service Prosecutions

EAT - Employment Appeal Tribunal

ECHR - European Convention on Human Rights

ECtHR - European Court on Human Rights

HA - Higher Authority

HMSO - Her Majesty's Stationery Office

JAG - Judge Advocate General

JEG - Justice Executive Group

JP - Justice of the Peace [a Magistrate]

JSCSC - Joint Services Command and Staff College

JSP - Joint Service Publication

MAA - Minor Administrative Action [in this paper to include, unless indicated otherwise, Major Administrative Action]

MCR - Magistrates' Courts Rules

MCS - Military Court Service

MCTC - Military Corrective Training Centre

MOU - Memoranda of Understanding

MP - Military police

MSL - Manual of Service Law

NAAFI - Navy, Army and Air Forces Institution

NCO - Non-commissioned Officer

NDA - Naval Discipline Act 1860

OACTU - Officer and Aircrew Training Unit [RAF College Cranwell]

OJAG - Office of the Judge Advocate General

PACE - Police and Criminal Evidence Act 1984

PNC - Police National Computer

QC - Queen's Counsel

RSM - Regimental Sergeant Major

SAC - Summary Appeal Court

SCC - Service Civilian Court

SCC - Service Complaints Commissioner

SCE - Service Children's Education

SJB - Service Justice Board

SJS - Service Justice System

SOFA - Status of Forces Agreements

SPA - Service Prosecuting Authority

SSAFA - Soldiers Sailors and Air Forces Families Association

SSVC - Services Sound and Vision Corporation

TSO - The Stationery Office [SPA]

UKAFSJS - United Kingdom Armed Forces Service Justice System

UNUDHR - United Nations Universal Declaration of Human Rights

BIBLIOGRAPHGY

Ames, J; 'Is prison the right place for autistic offenders?' [Times 1 June 2017]

Ashcroft, Lord, 'Veterans' Transition Review' [February 2014]

British Armed Forces Federation; [https://www.publications.parliament. uk/pa/cm 201213/cmselect/cmdfence/720/720vw02.htm].

Bower, T; 'Deceit, narcissism and chaos from the charmer who trashed Britain' Times News Review, 6 June 2016

Bourke, M; Russell Cooke, Solicitors, 2017

Brooke-Holland I; 'The Military Justice System: an introduction' [Standard Note SN06823 House of Commons Library 2012 [International Affairs and Defence section]

Bryman, A; 'Social Research Methods' 5th Ed.OUP 2016

Collie, J, Sir, Royal Institute of Public health; lecture on 'The Management of of Neurasthenia and Allied Disorders in the Army' June 14 1914

Doebbler, C. F; 'An Introduction to International Human Rights Law' 2006 [CD Publishing]

Eddy, J P; QC 'Scarlet and Ermine' Kimber, 1960,

Featherstone, D, 'All for a Shilling a Day' pp.8 & 9 [1966, Jarrolds, New English Library]

Gates, C; 'Disciplinary Uniformity in Uniform – A Success of the Human Rights Act 1988 ? Journal of Criminal Law Volume 72 issue 2/2008

Gavin, C, 'None Dare Call it Treason', [MW Books 1978]

Gibb, F. [See Ames]

Grieves; ECHR 57067/00 [Rant 1.17 p.6] 2003

Humphreys, C; QC 'Both Sides of the Circle' 1978, Buddhist Society Trust

Jepson, K; 'Army-discipline-often-equivalent-to-'kangaroo-courts' Link https://www.channel 4. com/news/army-discipline-often-equivalent-to-kangaroo-courts. [21 November 2012]

Kelly, J; Ministry of Justice Analytical Summary 2014 'The needs of ex-service personnel in the criminal justice system; Evidence from two surveys' [2014]

Kelsall, N UK Veterans One Voice [reported Mail March 2017]

Brooke-Holland, L. *'The Military Justice System: an introduction'* [Standard Note SN06823 House of Commons Library 2012 [International Affairs and Defence section]] stated [at 1.9 - Police records]

Morgan, R; Professor, Centre for crime & justice studies university of Bristol 'Summary justice - fast but fair?' August 2008

Morse, A Sir, National Audit Office 2017.

Mwedzi, P; 'De-mystifying the British Military Justice System' University of Lancashire November 2014

Nee, C, et al; The International Journal of Offender Therapy and Comparative Criminology [Addressing Criminality in childhood; is responsivity the Central Issue?] Nee, et al October 2012 [Sage]

Norton-Taylor, R; Guardian 02 October 2000 'Armed forces lose summary justice system'

Pigot, Captain, HM 'Hermione' 1797.

Rant, J; The Court Martial and Service Law [3rd edition, OU Press]

Rubin, G. R.; - 'Why Military law ? Some UK Perspectives'

Rodger, N.A.M.[Exeter University] 'The Command of the Ocean' p. 59, p. 452]. Penguin Books 2004.

Rojas, JPF; Daily Telegraph, 22 November 2012

Sassoon, S, *Memoirs of an Infantry Officer* 1931

Van Emden, R; 'The Road to Passchendaele' [Pen and Sword, 2017]

Supplementary Information

Critical Research Methods Evaluation

Introduction.

Research can be *objective*, i.e., monotheistic or physical tested characteristics, or *subjective*, i.e., idiographic or collected via observation and explanation [Swetman, 2015 p.31]. Both can be description and observation [*qualitative*] and concerned with measurement and numbers [*quantitative*].

The hypothesis ...

> ' *The Service summary justice process is unfair on the accused, as it does not follow the format of the civilian Magistrates' courts as regards inter alia, the rules of evidence, legal representation for the accused or being administered by legally qualified personnel ...*'

This raises questions [RQs] viz.,

Why does the Ministry of Defence [MOD] operate a system of summary justice which is not recognised by UK civilian courts?

Why does the same process apply equally in criminal cases and to non-criminal matters?

Why is a well-resourced Service organisation limited to military Courts Martial [CM] proceedings, and not utilised for all Service criminal matters?

Why were procedural errors highlighted by the European Court of Human Rights [ECtHR] and corrected in the CM process, not applied to the summary process in the 2016 review?

The first RQ encompasses the main element of the hypothesis, viz., when compared with civilian summary courts, the military process does not reflect the safeguards afforded the accused.

Regarding the second question, applying the same process to non-criminal matters, no civilian court empowered to hear criminal cases will ever deal with non-criminal, employment and disciplinary matters but within HM Forces such matters are dealt with by the same tribunal. In addition, a 'conviction' on disciplinary offence can be registered on the police national computer [PNC] but this does not apply to any civilian employment tribunal.

The Military Courts Service [MCS] comprises a substantial organisation, with the Directorate of Legal Services [RAF] alone having 29 different units in the UK and world-wide, although they do not just deal with service prosecutions.

The Judge Advocate General [JAG] Jeff Blackett, the senior Judge in the Armed Forces justice system, stated that ...

> '... the time when the criminal law could be easily assimilated and applied with a dash of common sense by unqualified people, even if of outstanding intelligence, has long passed'.
>
> [Rant on *The Court Martial and Service Law* at 1.09 p.4 [3rd edition Oxford University Press 08/2009].

This point, made eight years ago, is still not addressed and appears to represents wholesome support of a move to overhaul the current summary justice system and to remove it from the remit of unqualified staff. If this were to happen, the MCS would face a substantial criminal and disciplinary workload unless the summary justice system could deal effectively with non-criminal matters. This issue is addressed in the dissertation.

To the last question, the answer is supplied by the Service Justice Board [SJB] who state ..

> '...The Service Justice System is kept under regular review and ... is subject to parliamentary scrutiny every 5 years when the Armed Forces Act 2006 is renewed. The last such renewal was in 2016 during the passage of the Armed Forces Act. As the Act progressed through Parliament, key aspects of the system were scrutinised and debated and no significant changes to the system were made. However, the provisions of the Armed Forces Act 2006 will next need to be renewed by 2021 and we are already beginning to think about how best to use that opportunity to ensure our Service Justice System continues to meet the needs of our Armed Forces ...' [MOD UK, email, 06 July 2017]

This highlights an unsatisfactory situation, as Servicemen will face proceedings which might be unfair. Why there were no 'significant' changes to the SJS under the last review is not known, but one has to be optimistic that 'significant' changes will be made in the 2021 review, and the dissertation proposals will be available for the SJB to consider.

We have looked at what the research will endeavour to establish, now we have to consider the methods of achieving the aim.

Methodology.

The nature of this research is essentially *qualitative*, an emphasis on words embodying a view of social reality [Bryman, ibid] and the theory as set out in the hypothesis will be confirmed or otherwise by its findings; ergo, a *deductive* approach will apply as may be undertaken by anybody without any specialist knowledge.

The methodology comprises three parts, viz.,
What methods will be used;
Why they have been chosen and
Whether the methods can be implemented.
[Denscombe, 2012 p. 92]

The methodology is how the researcher will answer the questions to enable the drafting of the dissertation. As stated, his research is looking at a *system* set out, principally, in two main volumes, viz., the Act and the MSL which drives the *process* of summary justice. To investigate the hypothesis data will be collected by scrutiny of the following :-

The Manual of Service Law [MSL] and the Armed Forces Act 2006 [The Act]. These two volumes comprise virtually the entire source of the legislation governing the application of summary justice in HM Forces. These represent authoritative sources of information, published by the MOD. The Act is reviewed every five years, and although the last

review made no substantial changes it remains the current authority. In addition, using these and other equivalently sound sources, t
he font of the Service system, defeats any epistemological questions.

'Rant' on Courts Martial and Service Justice [3rd edition, 2009] [Ed. Blackett, J] This is a reference written for officers who deal with Forces justice, and it comments comprehensively on how ECtHR interventions have shaped the CM procedures. Although not carried through to the summary process, these interventions provide fertile ground for criticising the summary process. This authority raises no source or author issues and with 1 and 2 is a main reference for this research.

The Magistrates' Courts Rules 1981 [The Rules] provide the 'benchmark' against which the Service process will be compared, as it is these Rules which ensure as far as possible that the treatment of the accused is fair. The Rules are issued by the High Court therefore an unimpeachable reference.

Questionnaires, surveys and semi-structured Interviews with the Service Prosecution Authority [SPA], Military Court Service [MCS] and Judge Advocate General's Office represent secondary source analysis, with certain cost, time and quality advantages, [Bryman, 2016 p310]. Although it would be of some benefit to conduct some ethnographic research, and that it would 'illuminate' qualitative work [Sweetman, ibid p.37] and which may produce some interesting information, there are disadvantages in that we would need to [a] find and engage with a large number of serviceman who had been through the summary process and [b] deal with a substantial ethics problem and [c] it would be very time-consuming.

Further, as it is a *process* on trial here, the interviewees would not necessarily be authoritative, accurate and valid critics as would, for example, an officer who might have taken a substantial number of summary hearings, either as a Commanding Officer [CO] or as an Accused's Assisting Officer [AAO], and so have an intimate knowledge of the process but as they cannot be lawyers [refer the MSL and The Act], it cannot be assumed that they will have an appreciation of the issues this dissertation seeks to explore.

However, interviews with those who administer the system and are legally qualified to comment on any shortcomings, will qualify as valid, *inductive* primary research on the system under scrutiny, so enabling a derivation of sound theory from these sources. One such is the JAG [30th May 2017].

The use of questions administered to respondents, as well as in interviews, either structured [or *standardised interview*], or semi-structured interview [a *'general' form* of interview] had in this case to be limited to authorities, and although they all responded some referred to other authorities - a useful exercise in *'snowball sampling'* . [Bryman ibid.]. Some examples were the MSC referring to the MOD contacts for SJS review and to the Summary Justice departments; RAF College Cranwell OACTU officers referred to Coningsby and Waddington Support Services, Regional Legal Offices and the Forces Legal Advisor.

Notwithstanding, questionnaires and surveys raised particular problems because no interviewee can do more than express his authority's policy and cannot discourse on issues critical of other organisations.

As the researcher will have an idea of problems, he can phrase questions accordingly, but some answers will be references to the MSL, the Act or policy. The questionnaires can only address the interviewees' areas of interest. The rationale behind questionnaires is the need to know of any issues and how authority policies dealt with them.

Surveys can be expensive, with difficulties in the number of questions which could be asked, the way the questions are asked and whether the interviewees felt they could answer honestly or at all in view of their not wanting to be or appear to be voicing an opinion which 'bucks' Service policy.

RAF College Cranwell [Officers' Law Training] material will make interesting reading as, bearing in mind the complexity of the law, it will show how comprehensively the Officer Training syllabus covers this discipline. Where any officer can hold a summary hearing, it raises the question of whether he should be placed in that position without further training.

DVD - 'Advice and information for the accused' ArmySec-Group@MOD.uk comprises a simple overview of how a summary hearing is run and represents a valuable source of criticism when looked at from the point of view of fairness of the process. The source is the MOD.

The Joint Services Publication[JSP] 833 MOD 10/2008 and Queen's Regulations [QR] s1027 and Air Publication [AP] 3392 deals with more aspects of summary justice, MAAs and major admin. actions and are unimpeachable sources of information.

Some references to military law on the WWW deal with US systems of military justice, which it is inappropriate to investigate as in the UK we have adequate, alternative procedures in place to meet all SJS requirements. Postings of Morgan [University of Bristol], the National Audit Office and Mwedzi, University of Lancashire, are of value as is Brooke-Holland *'The Military Justice System: an introduction'* [Standard Note SN06823 House of Commons Library 2012 [International Affairs and Defence section] and will be referred to.

An unqualified internet source, unless verifiable, is of questionable value. Conversely, text-books and peer-reviewed papers are of value, but not absolutely so, as evidenced by the paper linking the measles, mumps and rubella [MMR] vaccine to autism and bowel disease. The author, Wakefield, A.J., a gastroenterologist and medical researcher, was eventually discredited. Hence, seeking a line of research to compliment another is to be encouraged.

Service Justice - an overview.

The Manual and The Act set out the two Service justice processes, viz., Courts Martial and summary justice. Examination of these two references, principally, will allow us to set out how the summary hearings work and only by comparing those findings with the civilian process permit us to highlight issues which make up the bulk of the dissertation content. The information in The Rules will be taken as setting out the fair process, and that is subject to the caveat that as it is a formula which governs the civilian process, and whereas it might not be regarded as entirely fair [in the sense that we can only look at bit from the viewpoint of the 'reasonable man'] it will be used as the yardstick for fairness.

Doubtless organisations such as Liberty will have different views on this concept of fairness, and conversely, the British Armed Forces Federation [BAFF] might also have certain views on the summary process, but this dissertation has to have a finite structure and will not therefore permit us to venture beyond what is only reasonable.

To answer the RQs, we have to look at the Service Justice [SJ] which comprises Courts Martial as managed by legally qualified personnel, and summary justice which is, as with minor administrative actions [MAA] and major [disciplinary] actions, also part of the summary process, managed by unqualified personnel; the MSL and The Act comprise the main reference for both.

Minor and major administrative actions are not mutually exclusive, but disciplinary action and MAA are, and as set out in JSP 833 MOD 10/2008. The disciplinary actions are in accordance with single-service policies, and, for the RAF, are as per the Queen's Regulations [QR] s1027 and Air Publication [AP] 3392 Vol. 5.

Service justice agencies are overseen by the MOD, with change brought about, as mooted above, by the SJB and the Justice Executive Group [JEG] [MCS, interview June 28 2017].

Hearings in the CM deal with serious disciplinary and criminal cases [MSL Ch. 6 and see also Rant at 5.18 p.83] and with appeals against a summary conviction or sentence or both.

The CM comprises a Judge Advocate who, with

between three and seven officers normally from the same service as the accused, make up 'the Board'. However, there are two cases which exposed flaws in the CM process. First was a 1997 case [Findlay-v-UK, ECHR 2210 and Rant, 1.20; 9.04] considered by the ECHR which went against the UK on the finding that the CM was not an independent and impartial tribunal, so violating the applicant's rights to a fair hearing under Article 6.1, and was referred to the ECtHR.

The second case is Martin-v-UK [ECHR 2006 4042/98 p.16 and Rant 5.206] which exposed the simple majority verdict as a severe weakness in the Service justice system and '*a striking contrast with the secure arrangements in the Crown Court'*.

Both cases brought about changes in the CM process. Perusal of the summary process, however, will discover these same flaws.

The civilian summary process.

Magistrates' Courts comprise a number of Magistrates or a single Judge, formerly a . Stipendiary Magistrate but since August 2000, by virtue of the Access to Justice Act 1999, are now 'District Judges [Magistrates' Court]'. All members of the Magistrates' Court are either qualified lawyers or have had training before they are permitted to sit. Whether Judges or Magistrates, performance falling below a certain standard will attract censure. The court process is adversarial. Counsel for the prosecution or defence are subject to the Bar Council rules, and Solicitors are regulated by the Solicitors' Regulatory Authority [SRA], and undergo compulsory continuing professional development [CPD] training.

The Rules have to be adhered to; they are complex and advocates will in all cases consider the *actus reus,* the elements of the offence, and will look for the *mens rea,* the guilty mind or criminal intention. For an offence to have been committed there must be a coincidence of both of these elements, i.e., *the act* and *the intent* [absolute liability offences excepted]. The prosecution will endeavour to demolish any defence. It is a continuous process.

Here is the issue; the civilian summary hearing process is based on the criteria set out above. The Service summary justice system is not based on these criteria; *ergo*, the proceedings appear *prima facie* unfair on the accused; but are they?
This is what this research has to establish if the hypothesis is to be proved.

The service summary process.

One must look at what study of the various research materials have produced thus far and consider how each of them, and how, collectively, they impact on the hypothesis. The main issues are as set out in the body of the dissertation.

One obvious point arising from the MSL, The Act and The Rules is that the process of law is not a simple one, and it is difficult to understand why, or more to the point, how, unqualified persons can assume the knowledge to control what is essential a court and to apply sanctions otherwise reserved to qualified personnel.

A service summary hearing is managed by an accused's CO, or a junior officer he nominates, who will be responsible for the process. He has jurisdiction in minor criminal and in disciplinary cases and his authority derives from the MSL and The Act. The offences he can try summarily are set out in MSL Chapter 6 Pt 4. Service police investigating an offence work in accordance with the Police and Criminal Evidence Act 1984 [PACE].

The MOD justify retaining the status quo by suggesting that military justice and civilian justice has to be different because of the nature of the Armed forces' role, and to an extent this might be true but there is a number of issues where the special nature of the serviceman's role cannot impinge on the administration of justice, so such an argument, if mooted, could in many cases, be specious.

Endeavouring to defending the indefensible might be an essential skill for litigation lawyers, but no researcher, if evidence-led, will find himself cornered by an interlocutor, but meandering into areas not researched, led perhaps by dogma, opinion or mere belief, a researcher could find himself embarrassed. It is not his beliefs the researcher should propound, but facts elicited through research.

What is the best kind of research?

This depends very much on the research topic. In this case it will be essentially *qualitative* and *deductive*, and this is made clear in perusing Bryman's Social Research Methods [Ibid].

Bibliography.

Access to Justice Act 1999, 'District Judges [Magistrates' Court]

Air Publication [AP] 3392 Vol. 5

Armed Forces Act 2006, The [MOD; The Stationery Office]

Brooke-Holland I; *'The Military Justice System: an introduction'* [Standard Note SN06823 House of

Bryman, A; *Social Research Methods;* [5th Edition OUP]
Commons Library 2012 [International Affairs and Defence section]

Denscombe, M; Research Proposals, 2012 [OUP]
Findlay -v-UK [1997 24 EHRR 2210

Jepson, K; *'Army-discipline-often-equivalent-to-'kangaroo-courts'* Link https://www.channel 4. com/news/army-discipline-often-equivalent-to-kangaroo-courts. [21 November 2012]

Manual of Service Law [MOD]

Morgan, R; Professor, Centre for crime & justice studies university of Bristol *'Summary justice - fast but fair ?'* August 2008

Mwedzi, P; *'De-mystifying the British Military Justice System'* University of Lancashire November 2014

Minor Administrative Actions [JSP 833 MOD 10/2008]

Police and Criminal Evidence Act 1984 [PACE].

Rant; *The Court Martial and Service Law* [3rd edition HHJ Jeff Blackett Oxford University Press 08/2009]

Queen's Regulations [QR] s1027
Sweetman, D; Writing your Dissertation 3rd edition 2015, Robinson

Wakefield, A.J MMR vaccine to autism and bowel disease.

Literature Review

Introduction.

The literature to be used in this Research comprises a substantial body of information extending to persons subject to Service law in any country in the world. There are two categories of persons subject to Service law, viz., Service personnel and ex-Service personnel [one category] and civilians subject to Service discipline [second category].

As simple as this sounds, the civilian category includes members of specific organisations such as the NAAFI, Service Children's Education, the Services Sound and Vision Corporation [SSVC], SSAFA, persons residing or staying with a person subject to Service law and Contractors on Deployed Operations [CODO].

Also included are civilians in HM ships [afloat] or aircraft [in flight]; note they do not have to be 'serving' personnel; persons in Service custody and Crown servants which usually means an MOD servant and members of specified military organisations working in any 'designated area' or anywhere if working for e.g., NATO. There are some other issues which make it a little more complicated and these are where there are certain protocols such as Status of Forces Agreements [SOFA] or Memoranda of Understanding [MOU] which can be applied by certain governments or regimes in other countries.

However, for the purposes of this research, interest extends only to serving personnel in any of HM forces in any country in the world and to the application of summary justice as applied by a person's commanding officer [CO] and, interesting as much of the literature relating to Service jurisdiction may be, and although this Review will refer to other situations, personnel and procedures, it is intended that the main thread running through this paper will be restricted to the central point as above.

Prosper Mwedzi in his article 'Demystifying the British Military Justice System' acknowledges that the Military Justice System ' ...exhibits some striking parallels to the Civilian justice system ... ' and in this he is correct but he states also that summary hearings were not within his remit so does not comment of the value or fairness of the Services summary justice process, where, as we will see, the barristers and solicitors he talks about getting involved, where they may have been of some benefit in the pursuit of fairness in disciplinary and criminal cases, are not invited to participate in summary hearings.

What he did mention was Findlay v The United Kingdom[1] and, bearing in mind the content of this review, it seems more probable that summary hearings are even less 'independent and impartial' than Courts Martial. The same comment would apply to Chris Gates 'Disciplinary Uniformity in Uniform – A Success of the Human Rights Act 1988?[2] who regrettably ignores the SJ process.

---

1   (110/1995/616/706) 25 February 1997: independence and impartiality of court-martial; Convening officer central to prosecution and closely linked to prosecuting authorities
2   Journal of Criminal Law Volume 72 issue 2 2008

This seems unfair, as even this process can have long-lasting effects on the individual, not only whilst he is serving, but also once he has been discharged into civilian life after a full career in HM forces.

The Literature.
The documents which will be used in this research are as follows;

1. The Service Justice System – an overview.

2. Armed Forces Act [AFA]

3. Notes to AFA

4. Manual of Service Law
Ch. 1 - Introduction
Ch. 2 - Meaning of Commanding Officer
Ch. 3 - Jurisdiction and time limits
Ch. 4 - Arrest and search, stop and search, entry search and seizure, and retention.
Ch. 5 - Custody
Ch. 6 - Investigation, charging and MODe of trial
Ch. 7 - Non-criminal conduct [disciplinary] offences
Ch. 8 - Criminal conduct offences
Ch. 9 - Summary hearing and activation of suspended sentences of Service detention
Ch. 10 - Absence and desertion
Ch. 11 - Summary hearing – dealing with evidence
Ch. 12 - Defences, mitigation and criminal responsibility
Ch. 13 - Summary hearing sentencing and punishments
Ch. 14 - Commanding officers' guide to sentencing at summary hearing
Ch. 15 - Summary hearing review and appeal

Ch. 27[3] - The Summary Appeal Court

5. Minor Administrative Action

6. Rights for accused under the Service Justice System

7. Support Available for Service Personnel arrested or charged with offences under the SJS

8. Magistrates' Courts Procedure

9. The Magistrates' Courts Rules

Review.
Document 1.

An overview of the Service Justice System [4] and the Armed Forces Act [the Act][5].

This document is a short brief produced by the Armed Forces Bill team at the Ministry of Defence [MOD] and comprises five pages which, although not a detailed overview of the Service Justice System [SJS] does comprise a very broad outline of the legal framework within which the Services operate.
It points out that the SJS is ' ... *constructed to provide a mechanism which those accused of disciplinary offences are dealt with fairly, quickly and have a right to appeal against their sentence* ...'.

---

3   Chapters 16 to 26 cover aspects of Service Law which are not the subject of this research for example, Financial penalty renouncement orders, Naval chaplains, powers of officers to take affidavits etc.
4   The SJS harmonises the single-Service discipline Acts
5   Armed Forces Act 2006 took effect 31 October 2009

This does not say appeal against 'conviction' and whether this was a deliberate omission is not known but bearing in mind the very substantial body of material available on the SJS it is probably of no consequence.

It also outlines the key principles underlying the Act which provide, inter alia, that this system of Service law should be fair and be seen to be so, is efficient, transportable [used anywhere in the world] and compliant with the European Court of Human Rights [ECHR] legislation.

A person's CO sits at the heart of the discipline [summary justice] process, as it is he who has control of his unit – whether it is a small overseas unit, a temporary or permanent detachment, which can comprise anything from half a dozen personnel or several hundred, or a complete Army, Navy or RAF station in the UK.

The point of special interest in this brief missive, is that it states ' Commanders are best placed to understand the service environment ….[etc.] ' and with the very recent business about Philip Shiner's practice, Public Interest Lawyers and that of Leigh Day, where some characters were encouraged to dredge up - under the Government-funded Iraq Historic Allegations Team [IHAT] - some cases of [alleged] misconduct by the Armed Forces and which resulted in some 3,600 case- files being opened, and the very current case of Marine 'A' who shot and killed an injured enemy combatant. Although the latter was not a summary justice case, it does have a place for a brief mention here.

It did inter alia raise the point about servicemen being dealt with by civilian courts for battlefield misdemeanours as an issue, in particular about it being easy to ignore factors which have a bearing on conduct in question and which if considered will or could bring about a very different result.

In the case of Marine 'A', a verdict of murder was passed down, when the facts seemed to indicate that a conviction for manslaughter was probably more appropriate.

Empirical evidence indicates that the prosecution is hardly likely to suggest – even in conference with the defence – that a lesser charge could be considered. It is pointless to expand here on this prosecution / defence relationship, but suffice it to say that this Marine 'A' case will probably open up a can of worms for many legal professionals to mull over.

However, the point is made; the CO deals with the administration of summary justice, a serviceman dealing with servicemen and who is fully aware of many factors known only to people who are serving and who have served and often under very difficult circumstances.

In addition, there are certain offences [disciplinary offences] mentioned in this Overview which only apply to armed forces personnel, but which must nevertheless be dealt with fairly.
Overall, this document gives a broad outline and in simple terms, of how the SJS works and many of the issues mentioned are dealt more comprehensively in further documents.

Document 2.

Armed Forces Act [the Act] 2006 Chapter 52

The Act came into effect on 31 October 2009 and represents the first major overhaul of service law for half a century. In 19 parts, plus 17 schedules, it is a comprehensive document which replaces the old Air Force Act of 1955, the Army Act 1955 and Navy Discipline Act of 1957.

Part one lists offences and, understandably, many are exclusive to service personnel such as mutiny, neglect of duty, offences against service justice and issues relating to ships and aircraft.

There will be many references to this document throughout this review.

Document 3.

The Explanatory Notes to the AFA 2006.

This forms part of essential reading for all purposes related to the AFA but do not form part of the Act and neither have they been endorsed by Parliament. Notwithstanding, the reviewer has highlighted as of particular interest the Introduction, the Background[6] and the Overview of the Act[7] and Structure of The Act[8] which provides a concise albeit short précis for a casual enquirer into the Act and the remaining 125 pages are an interesting voyage into the Service justice system and an adequate introduction for all but the most serious prosecutor or offender who will have to engage with The Act and its near cousin the Manual of Service Law.

---

6   Both on page 1
7   Page 3
8   Pages 4 to 6

Document 4.
The Manual of Service Law [MSL]

The MSL is published to provide policy guidance and reference material on the AFA and comprises three volumes and it is volume one chapters one to 15, as listed above, and Volume two, chapter 27, of which only The Court Guide, and 'The Summary Appeal Court' apply. Volume three is a Legal Compendium, then come forms and leaflets. The booklet ' Your rights if you are accused ' as at number nine above is also of interest.

The MSL is a truly substantial work, running to 35 chapters, unfortunately only available by downloading from the MOD web. HMSO / The Stationery Office [TSO] do not print it as they do the Armed Forces Act. The sections appropriate to this research amount in all to 16 of the chapters, some 600 pages. Much of the material needed is buried in various paragraphs within almost all of those volumes, and eliciting the essential information is a substantial task.

Chapter one is a brief résumé of what the MSL contains, covering the background to the Act, what The Act covers and governance and stresses that COs are at the '...*very heart of the SJS with appropriate disciplinary and administrative powers over all personnel under their command'*..... It is clear that these officers who administer summary justice [as opposed to that dispensed by the Courts Martial] must have, at the very minimum, a basic grasp of Service law and how to apply it.

This presupposes that they undertake some training. However, it does not necessarily mean that they use their powers in a way which a civilian court, staffed by law professionals, would do, and is indeed obliged to do. As this chapter points out, there are two distinct streams which apply to service justice; the first - Service law - creates additional offences which are exclusively of a Service nature and that the law applies wherever in the world the serviceman is serving.

It is this issue which lies at the heart of this research, and a point which will be pursued through the substantial number of documents available to the researcher.

Chapter two 'Meaning of commanding officer' and how a serviceman's CO is identified under Defence Council regulations[9] and how an officer, i.e., the holder of the Queen's commission, must be able to identify as being a person's CO as it is in him the Act invests the power to deal with servicemen, sub-units, attached personnel and some civilians ['relevant civilians'][10] all of whom are described within the MSL.

The CO is under a duty to promulgate any delegation of his powers, to know who his higher authority [HA] is, being the CO's superior officer, who in turn should know who his own COs are. In realty therefore, there is always a person who is at any time and in any situation invested with the authority to administer summary justice under the Act, and which is a fundamental requirement in the process.

---

9   The Armed Forces [Meaning of Commanding Officer] Regulations 2009
10 See chapter 2 MSL

Chapter 3 covers jurisdiction and time limits and the bulk of this chapter deals with those who are subject to service law, and for civilians subject to service law any Service offence will be tried by the Service Civilian Court [SCC], where not to be tried by court martial [CM]. Murder, manslaughter, causing the death of a child, firearms offences and a few others are all CM offences.

Summary hearings

A CO, or an empowered subordinate commander, can hear cases which are capable of being dealt with summarily, clearly, and committed by any person subject to Service law. The CO can hear cases and depending on the accused's rank, the CO's power of punishment[11], the meaning of commanding officer and investigation and mode of trial[12] but a CO cannot hear a charge against a civilian [or charge a civilian with an offence] and these cases will either be referred to the Director of Service Prosecutions [DSP] and heard either by the SCC or by CM – or a CO can decide to take no action[13]. As we are not concerned with civilian matters, very little of this process is of interest.

Appellate courts.

The Summary Appeal Court [SAC] has jurisdiction to hear an appeal from a summary hearing and this is comprehensively covered in chapter 18 MSL.

The rest of chapter three deals with choice of

---

11 Chapter 13 MSL - Summary hearing, sentencing and punishments.
12 Chapter 6 MSL - Investigation, charging and mode of trial
13 S. 121/2 and 52/3 &4 AFA

jurisdiction, jurisdiction as to time, double jeopardy and some transitional guidance. It also suggests that if a matter has been heard by way of ' Minor Administrative Action' [MAA[14] - Joint Service Publication [JSP] 833 MOD] then it cannot be revisited by a summary hearing. MAAs are, however, also dealt with summarily and is a convenient way of disposing of small disciplinary hiccoughs but unfortunately there is a real danger that they are used inappropriately. An example – a real case – will be cited in the Research Thesis.

Chapter 4 comprises some 47 pages, covering arrest and search, stop and search, entry search and seizure, and retention. There is a number of annexes principally forms, receipts and notices all of which have a relevance to the main content of this chapter. As with a substantial amount of information, this research cannot dwell on such issues as this would be an excursion into areas too wide to deal with here and with little bearing on the conduct of the summary hearings with which we are mainly concerned.

Chapter 5 covers custody. This is of some interest as how a person is treated in custody [especially within the Armed Forces for various reasons concerning the nature of the custody staff usually junior NCOs] could result in an outcome wholly or partially different if the accused had been treated correctly.

The individual can normally be held for 48 hours, and also has a right to nominate a person to be his AAO[15] to be his 'assisting officer' and this can be a

---

14 See document 5
15 But not a legally-qualified person except a RN lawyer acting as a

Service person of certain rank. The AAO cannot be a lawyer.

This disqualification of lawyers [a recurring theme in service law] is of concern as empirical evidence indicates that, even in some serious cases, the defence lawyer will often suggest that the accused pleads guilty, when for example, he is convinced by his legal professional that is the better course under the circumstances. There is nothing to suggest that the same practice is not followed on occasions by the AAO and for diverse reasons. This will be addressed at length in the thesis.

Overall, this chapter is a one which will require scrutiny and any deviation from the rules set out may well be, if properly documented, a point for the summary court to account for and which may involve undue influence or maltreatment by the custodians. However, the 'Assisting Officer' could be involved and further points on this appointment are certainly relevant and will be aired in full in the thesis but overall, the custody provisions seem comprehensive and should under normal circumstances provide no causes for concern if properly effected.

Chapter 6. This is another substantial document, and gets to the heart of this research. It is titled 'Investigation, Charging & Mode of trial' and is some 70 pages in length with annexes A to S. With the aim of the research comprising a comparison of the application of summary justice by Magistrates' courts and that as administered by the force's personnel, it is a valuable document and one which will be referred to throughput the thesis.

'divisional officer'.

The chapter aims to be guidance for those responsible for administering discipline, the investigation, selection and charging and deciding on the mode of trial and comprises seven parts, General principles, Offences overview, Investigation, Offences which can be heard summarily, a section on CM or the SCC [which we do not need to deal with] and finally Administrative and Welfare responsibilities.

Statutory provisions relating to investigation and charging are covered in the Act[16].

The general principles set out the procedure where an offence has been committed, is very much like the civilian process. There is an investigation either by the CO or by the military [service] police[17] ; it is the CO who decides on whether there should be an investigation, and who should do it, which depends on the seriousness of the matter, its complexity and whether, if committed, it can be tried summarily.

Some offences have to be referred to the Director of Service Prosecutions [DSP][18] but other than those, the reports are sent to the accused's CO when a charge may be suggested. The CO has the authority to either deal with the case summarily, to refer to the DSP or take no action or deal with it administratively[19].

---

16 Sections 113 to '28 and Pt v5 of the AFA 2009 and at volume 3 of the MSL [the legal compendium]

17 Service police – Royal navy Police, Royal Military Police or the Royal Air Force Police- see section 375[1] of The Act

18 Any offence listed in schedule 2 to The Act or relates to prescribed circumstances

19 Administrative Action ; Ch 3 Page 1-3-28 MSL; and see document 5 [below]

A charge is brought when the CO signs the charge sheet and hands a copy to the accused.
So far so good; the process more or less follows procedures similar to those of a normal civilian police investigation, with the obvious difference that in the civilian cases it is usually the Director of Public Prosecutions DPP] who decides if a case is to be pursued.

Another similarity is that if, during a summary hearing, the CO finds he has insufficient power to deal with the case, and before any finding is made, he can refer it to the DSP to deal with. This is similar to the Magistrates committing a case to the crown courts, and in those cases, there can be a full 'committal' hearing before a committal to the crown court, or just a simple committal with no hearing.

There is, however, no formal hearing before a CO assigns to a CM, just a CO review of the case before he makes any decision so, effectively, the defence do not get the opportunity to rehearse their case as some solicitors and barristers like to do in the lower, civilian, courts, where they think it to be of some value to their case to test their evidence and [doubtless] obtain some clarification on any obviously unhelpful - or possibly - helpful matters before the crown court hearing.

Part two of this chapter, Offences Overview, sets out in in various Annexes, the offences and how they can be tried. Annex B to this chapter – mainly disciplinary offences for example, looting, absence without leave, disobedience to lawful commands, ill-treatment of subordinates, some 30 in all, can be dealt with summarily[20]. Summary disposal can apply to more serious offences [listed at Annex C[21] to this chapter] provided the CO has permission from HA.

Schedule 2 offences[22], such as serious disciplinary offences which covers mutiny and desertion, and criminal offences such as murder and manslaughter and serious sexual offences must all be tried by CM. These, therefore, will not be part of this research.

Concurrent jurisdiction can also be an issue. Some cases can be investigated or prosecuted by Service, civilian or foreign authorities taking into account the SOFA or MOU protocols[23].

Overall, this chapter provides a comprehensive guide to investigation and mode of trial, and at all stages the welfare of accused and any assistance he may need is usually available. However, and as already mooted, a main point for investigation is the level of competence of any AAO appointed to the accused, his level of knowledge and his suitability for the role inter alia. In many cases he may be appointed – or selected – only because he is known to the accused in some other capacity.

Chapter 7. This is the largest chapter in the MSL, comprising about 200 pages, and covers non-criminal conduct. It is essential to understand that there is a substantial number of service offences which are non-criminal but, notwithstanding, to be charged with any of these offences can be as

---

20 Where there is an attempt to commit an offence, the Co may hear provided it is not an attempt to commit any criminal offence
21 For example, assault occasioning ABH, possession of an offensive weapon or any attempt etc.
22 At Annex D
23 See Introduction [above]

traumatic and far-reaching for the serviceman as any criminal offence proceedings can be for him [or a civilian] so the way they are investigated and dealt with summarily and even though principally disciplinary offences, the procedures is still of importance to this research as every step in the process has to be and has to be seen to be fair.

As an aside, and for historical interest only, they include 'failure to escape' [shades of Colditz] and 'prize' offences committed by an officer in command of a ship or aircraft. The latter has its origins in the days of Nelson and earlier, when our own Navy captains were encouraged to capture 'enemy 'prize' ships, and it should be remembered that most of the 'prize' proceeds finished up in the pockets of anybody but the sailors who made the capture, even though some captains did fairly well. [As an interesting excursion into Naval history look up Cochrane [in particular] and Fisher and Benbow]

The chapter sets out for each of the [many] offences, and comprehensively, the AFA reference, the type of offence, a specimen charge, the ingredients of the offence, defences and notes [essentially further guidance and alternative charges]. As an example, set out below is a specimen case [although 'dangerous flying' sounds more interesting than 'low flying' the former is unfortunately an offence which cannot be tried summarily so here a case of low flying is offered].

Example:

34 Low Flying:
A person subject to service law commits an offence if (a) he flies an aircraft at a height of less than the minimum height other than

(i) when taking off or landing or (ii) in any other circumstance prescribed by regulations made by the Defence Council; and (b) he intends to fly, or is reckless as to whether he flies, the aircraft at a height less than the minimum height, or he is negligent.

If a person flies an aircraft in contravention of subsection (1) on the orders of another person who is in command of the aircraft, that other person is for the purposes of this section treated as flying the aircraft.

In this section 'minimum height' means the height prescribed by regulation made by the Defence Council.

A person guilty of an offence under this section is liable to any punishment mentioned in the Table in section 164, but any sentence of imprisonment imposed in respect of the offence must not exceed two years.

AFA 06 s.34

1.   Type of offence

An offence under this section may be heard summarily[24]

2.   Specimen charge

UNLAWFUL LOW FLYING CONTRARY TO SECTION 34(1) OF THE ARMED FORCES ACT 2006

[DC] on 22 May 2010 when pilot of Her Majesty's aircraft XR677 intentionally flew the said aircraft at a height of less than the 2,000 feet minimum

---

24 Section 53 of the Act

prescribed limit in Ministry of Defence Military Aircraft Regulations made by the Defence Council or was reckless as to whether the said aircraft was being flown below 2,000 feet.

3.   Ingredients of the offence
A person subject to Service Law

For persons subject to Service law see Chapter 3 [Jurisdiction and time limits]

Aircraft
or the purposes of offences under this section aircraft are defined under section 374 of the Act

Minimum height
A fixed wing aircraft will low fly for the purposes of the charge if without authorisation it is flown below 2,000 feet above the ground of other surface. A rotary wing aircraft { including light propeller aircraft) will fly low if without authorisation it is flown at a height below 500 feet above the ground or other surface[25]. The minimum height and the circumstances in which a pilot will have authorisation to fly below these are set out in regulation 4 of Low Flying Regulations 2009.

When taking off or landing
This will include practice approaches where the aircraft descends as it to land but does not in fact do so.
Any other circumstance prescribed by regulations
See regulation 4 of Low Flying Regulations 2009

Intends
For intention generally see Chapter 12 (Defences,

---

25 Low Flying Regulations 2009 regulation 3 and JSP 550

mitigation and criminal responsibility)
Reckless
For recklessness generally see Chapter 12 (
Defences, mitigation and criminal responsibility)

Negligently
For negligence generally see Chapter 12 (
Defences, mitigation and criminal responsibility)

4.   Defences

For defences generally see Chapter 12 (Defences, mitigation and criminal responsibility) A pilot may have a defence if he can show that he was low flying under the orders of another person in command of the aircraft. The other person who is in command of the aircraft may be charged with an offence under this section.

5.   Notes

Other offences may be considered.
If the low flying occurred over an area where the pilot had previous associations e.g., home, school evidence to this fact may be produced though this in itself would not be sufficient to justify a conviction. Where low flying occurred without prior permission e.g. to avoid adverse weather conditions and it was not reported but where it was practical to report it. Before bringing a charge under this section consider JSP 550 [Military Aviation Policy Regulations and Directives]
Every offence dealt with in chapter seven is individually set out in similar form, so not only the CO but all the individuals in the prosecuting chain can set out clearly the full details of the offence in preparation for charging the accused and the subsequent hearing if indeed it proceeds that far.

This is fair on both parties, prosecution and for the accused.

Chapter 8. This chapter deals with Service[26] personnel who commit criminal offences some of which can be dealt with summarily and others dealt with summarily but only with permission from HA. They include offences of violence, dishonesty, road traffic offences miscellaneous offences and section 43 to 48 of the Armed Forces Act 2006 offences – attempting, conspiring , inciting, aiding, abetting, counselling or procuring criminal conduct.

Each of the offences listed has been set out in tabular form and, as with chapter seven above and with the same advantages.

There is little need therefore to review this chapter any more than has already been set out.

Chapter 9. Summary hearing and activation of suspended sentences of Service detention. It is this chapter which is of most interest to the research, and it throws up a number of troubling points.
Part 1 – Delegations and applications to HA;
Part 2 - Preliminary procedures for a summary hearing;
Part 3 – General considerations for summary hearing and preliminary actions, including where activation of suspended sentences of detention may be required;
Part 4 covers procedures where a charge is denied;
Part 5 where the charge is admitted.
Parts 6,7,8 and 9 deal with post hearing, elections

---

26 Where Service personnel are mentioned it should always be read to include 'relevant civilians'

for CM and activation of a suspended sentence of detention – imposed either by a CO or by a Summary Appeal Court [SAC] - where an offender is subsequently convicted of an offence in the British Isles by a civilian court or by a CO.

The above represents the substantial degree of power invested in a CO or another [delegated] officer authorised by him and should surely indicate that all hearings are fair and compare well with the civilian court processes.

However, there is a number of issues which should be addressed.

At introduction, paragraph two, it states ' Summary discipline enables the chain of command to exercise effective authority in all situations including on operations. It provides procedures under which Service offences, criminal and non-criminal [disciplinary] conduct offences, can be dealt with swiftly and fairly in support of operational effectiveness'.

At paragraph three; 'A summary hearing is an inquisitorial process [*Researcher's note - A system employed by some foreign countries under which the Judge decides the scope and range of the hearing, searches for the facts listens to witnesses, examines documents and orders that evidence be taken after which he makes further investigations if he considers them necessary* [27]].

There is no prosecutor as such to present the case and in a contested case the Judge [or officer in our cases] determines the facts of the case based on

---

27 Dictionary of Law L B Curzon; 6th edition

the evidence from the accused and from the witnesses. In parts of Europe where this system operates it is a Judge [*huge d'instruction*] and not a layman who manages this process.

The conduct of summary hearings – sentencing and punishments[28] sets out the procedures to be followed, the factors that should be considered when sentencing and guidance on punishments.

For summary hearing review and appeal[29] again, the procedures are set out for when an offender wishes to appeal to the Summary Appeal Court [SAC]. All this is unique to the Service Justice System [SJS].

For a summary hearing, the CO – or authorised person – will prepare a summary of evidence and will also inform the accused of his rights which are that he can elect court martial [CM] trial, to be represented, to question witnesses, to give evidence, to provide evidence of his own witnesses and – after the summary hearing – to appeal to the SAC.

The CO will also have the disciplinary record of the accused before the summary hearing commences,

The accused will be advised of his rights where the question of activation of suspended sentences arises. However, this is not an aspect which will be covered in the research.

The general impression is that, with certain limits, every effort is made to assist the offender but a

---

28 Chapter 13
29 Chapter 15

closer look at the provisions set out in this chapter shows that he has to labour under a number of disadvantages.

Although the CO has to inform the accused that he is entitled to seek legal advice, and which is a matter he is advised to discuss with any AAO[30] appointed to help the accused through the summary process, any legal advice has to be at the accused's expense. There are many solicitors firms willing to offer free advice, but one has to consider that the advice offered on a pro bono basis [not something many lawyers are known for] basis will not be anything like as comprehensive as the accused may need, and sooner or later the advice will come with a pretty hefty fee attached, and empirical evidence suggests a level of about £200 per hour.

Alternatively, legal aid may be available; this is discussed in full below. In addition, a staff lawyer may be approached for assistance. However, *a lawyer[31] is not allowed to be present during summary hearings.*

Representation may, however, be via the AAO; a person can be appointed as an AAO provided they are a service person, they are of a certain minimum rank and they consent to the nomination. He cannot be a lawyer[32] If a suitable person cannot be found by the accused then the CO will offer a selection

---

30 AAO – Accused Assisting Officer

31 Lawyer – can be a solicitor or a barrister retired or otherwise; however, the term now seems to include any person engaged within the law and could [loosely interpreted] include an articled clerk, a FILEX, a licensed conveyancer et al; however we must assume the legislation meant a barrister or solicitor [the latter with or without a current practising certificate]

32 But see footnote 9

from which the accused can pick his AAO. After nomination, the minimum time of 24 hours must elapse before any hearing can begin. An AAO cannot be a subordinate commander who may have previously heard evidence against the accused, unit's administrative staff who have been dealing with the case, a person who may be called as a witness or lawyers.

As positive as this sounds, it does impose a very important duty on the AAO, and one which opinion might suggest is too much of a burden for any unqualified person. The 'brief for a nominated AAO runs to seven pages.

The duty involves:-

Seeking legal advice if in any doubt as to the case or any of his duties;
He has to understand the charge [from the charge sheet the accused will have been given by his CO];

Understand the procedures e.g., to be aware of the summary hearing procedures;

Ensure the accused also understands the process and take him through the booklet 'Rights for accused under the Service Justice System [SJS];

Advise him that he can seek legal advice;
Ensure that the accused is aware that the conviction could be recorded on the Police National Computer [PNC]; on this see infra and that he may have to give a DNA sample and have his fingerprints taken if found guilty;

That if the accused disputes any allegations [it says 'facts' which is probably a typo; facts are facts and cannot be in dispute] then the AAO should consider which witnesses can be used to provide relevant evidence;

During the hearing the AAO should 'insure' [sic] that the AAO or the accused question any witnesses where it would be in the accused's interest to do so;
Accused's evidence – the AAO should help the accused to decide whether to give evidence at the appropriate time and whether oral or written;

Ask the accused if there is any evidence or witnesses who will assist his case. The AAO should then ' assess the evidence and select those witnesses who best support the accused's case'.

Read to the CO any written submissions;

Question the witnesses;

Collect statements in mitigation if a finding of guilt is registered.
As already suggested, all this represents an onerous task for a layman, maybe even for an articled clerk and for many solicitors, but for a layman it means venturing into the rules of evidence, having to represent the accused under what could be very intimidating circumstance in the presence of senior officers.
This is a role not to be taken lightly and the burden of the shoulders of the AAO is substantial with far-reaching consequences for the accused if he fails in his duty to carry out effectively those tasks.

This is a matter which will feature prominently in the research thesis.

Returning to the Police National Computer [PNC]; at Annex Q to volume 1 chapter 9 JSP 830 MSL [this current chapter] comprises 4 pages of offences capable of being heard at summary level, and whether they are recordable on the PNC. Offence; Misconduct towards a senior officer – actual misconduct and attempts are recordable, but only if under s. 11(1) AFA which is using violence against a senior officer knowing he is a senior officer.

Also recordable are s. 24 offences – damage or loss of public or Service property, s. 27 obstructing or failing to assist a Service policeman, s. 28 resistance to arrest, s. 29 offences in relation to Service custody, s. 30(1) negligently doing an act that results in a person's escape or s. 30(2) allowing an escape or unlawful release of prisoners etc. All criminal offences able to be heard summarily [Pt 2 Schedule 1 of AFA] and attempts are recordable.

With some of the above one must ask ... Why? How can offences committed within HM forces, where the Serviceman may be working at the time of the offence under pressures and conditions far removed from those of a civilian's way of life?

In all, the content of this chapter raises many issues which deserve closer investigation.

Chapter 10. Absence and desertion. Not of any value to this research.

Chapter 11. Summary hearing – dealing with evidence. This states the intention to provide the CO and his staff with the ability to recognise issues which may arise during a hearing and to establish the facts and recognise when to seek staff legal advice.

This seeking of staff advice is a recurring theme, and it is worth looking at, firstly, whether this is a need because the CO *et al* does not appreciate the basic rules of evidence and secondly just how long this process takes bearing in mind the fundamental principle of the SJS is '*to provide a mechanism which those accused of disciplinary offences are dealt with fairly, quickly ...*'

However, this chapter goes on to say that the summary hearing is not a court; it is an inquisitorial process [see footnote 21] in which the CO *endeavours* to discover the facts by actively searching for evidence and questioning the witnesses and that '*no rules of evidence as such apply but the principles ensure both best practice and fairness to the accused* '.

This is another valuable point for research – does it indeed offer *best practice and fairness* for the accused.

However, and after a discussion on witness evidence which is also an important issue to consider – in particular its presentation to the hearing and the obvious limitations which seem inherent in this system – there is a note about documentary evidence and rules relating to the origin and relevance of the documents which the CO should seek to apply because the Summary Appeal Court [SAC] will require documentary evidence to be produced in a certain form *to make it legally admissible.*

The more one considers the content of this chapter, the more issues seem to arise; for example, If it is up to the CO entirely to decide the value of evidence, without adhering strictly to the rules of evidence, then why is the documentary evidence the apparent exception?

It then goes on to look at real and circumstantial evidence, burden and standard of proof, relevance and admissibility of evidence.

In all, there is an indication that in fact, and contrary to the opening paragraphs, many of the Rules of Evidence should apply. And what of the safeguards offered by PACE or its Codes [e.g.; R v Canale[33] and R v Latif and Shahzad[34]] - would the CO have accepted that evidence?

Chapter 12. Defences, mitigation and criminal responsibility are set out and doubtless the CO will be aware of them. However, where the accused or his AAO does not appreciate the value of any information where a good defence could apply, there will obviously be issues. It has already been stated above that the burden on the AAO is quite a heavy one – especially that a hearing can commence 24 hours after his appointment; will he be able to ask for more time ? Indeed, he can but he may feel pressured into agreeing too early a date for the hearing when he may not be 'up to speed' with his duties.

Another issue of concern is the plea in mitigation; this is not a complex undertaking, but nevertheless it is important and again, the art of advocacy is not easily acquired and both the accused and the AAO may find great difficulty in presenting their case

---

33 1990 – evidence not accepted as noted not contemporaneously written up
34 A police officer's conduct criminal and deceitful

convincingly whether during the hearing before a case is 'proved or disproved' - taken loosely - and any subsequent mitigation plea if appropriate.

Part 3 of this chapter devotes three pages to criminal responsibility – intention, recklessness, negligence, lawful or reasonable excuse and the burden of proof. In legal textbooks, these points take up numerous chapters.

Chapter 13. Summary hearing, sentencing and punishments, which sets out the purpose of sentencing and includes punishment, discipline, crime reduction by deterrence, reform and rehabilitation, protection of both public and servicemen, reparation and welfare[35] A period in detention is supposed to do more or less the same as a civilian prison is supposed to do but with obvious differences one being that the maximum term of detention [the Service calls it 'detention'] which can be handed down [with HA] is 90 days.

The chapter also sets out a number of factors indicating higher culpability or harm which are specific to the Service i.e., common offence in unit, operational environment and experience of the service person or in a position or responsibility, involvement of alcohol, adverse effect on Service discipline and 'being in the public eye'. However, some punishments are reserved for officers [forfeiture of seniority] ; for officers and non-commissioned officers [corporals, sergeants etc.] admonishments and reprimands; other ranks - detention, reduction in rank and fines. There is no explanation as to why, but it is another issue to pursue as it seems on the face of it to be inherently

---

35 For offenders aged 18 or under

unfair.

There would be no equivalent discrimination in the Magistrates' courts, where all punishments are available [at least, up to the maximum sentence of 6 months in prison] and in Service summary hearing the most that can be handed down is, as above, 90 days 'detention' which equates to six months [where only half the sentence will be served in a civilian prison].

Annex C to this chapter has an interesting note about the military corrective training centre – rehabilitative training [MCTC]. Detainees are either 'A' or 'D' company; 'A' company undergo a programme of military training under a regime based on reward for effort and most respond to become better service personnel. In 'D' company there is access to education and skills workshops and City & Guilds qualifications and lessons in IT.

Perhaps the MoJ could look at this programme as a way of reducing the very high rate [50% +] of recidivism in civilian prisons.

The point of this is to indicate that even the worst of the detainees within the Service are in fact well looked after, albeit in a more hostile regime that would ever be tolerated by HMPS. The same applies to pre-hearing treatment as will have been seen from the above, and with this there is no argument except that the summary hearing process leaves, as is indicated so far, a lot to be desired.

Full information on sentencing powers and mandatory etc. sentences is as set out in Part 8 AFA.

Chapter 14. The Summary hearing and sentencing guide – in its introduction states ' The impartial administration of discipline is essential to the morale and cohesion of a Service unit [and] fairness at summary hearings generates confidence in other aspects of unit management'.

This is a laudable approach, but this research is to question whether in fact, the summary hearing / process is fair. Therefore, this literature review will not dwell on the sentencing aspect, except in so far as has been alluded to in the above chapter.

The guide in this chapter sets out in clear, tabular form the offence and mitigating factors, so there is very little room for the CO to err so far from the guide that an immediate reference can be made to the SAC [Summary Appeal Court].

Taking, as an example, the low flying issue referred to above[36]. This is as follows :
s.34 AFA06 Low flying contrary to s 34 Armed Forces Act 2006

Charging Reference
MSL Chapter 7 Non-criminal conduct [disciplinary] offences p1-7-104
Mitigating factors
Distraction Impulsive action No damage or distress caused No intention; Genuine remorse.

Aggravating factors
Very low height Serious deviation from authorised height Pilot in executive position; damage / injury caused; carrying ordnance.

---

36 See chapter 7.

Range of punishments
Punishment after denial of offence:
Low – reprimand / fine; Entry point – severe
reprimand and up to 14 days fine; High – Forfeiture
of seniority and severe reprimand, reduction in rank
for NCO aircrew up to 28 days fine

Punishment after admission of offence
Low – Admonition / reprimands; Entry point – Up to
10 days fine; severe reprimands; High – Up to 14
days fine or forfeiture of seniority, reduction in rank
for NCO aircrew

Sentencing guide
Sentencing must contain a large element of
deterrence for such a risky activity particularly if the
offender was in a position of authority.

Chapter 15. It is of some comfort perhaps that the
findings of a summary hearing may be reviewed by
the Defence Council or an officer appointed for this
purpose [The Reviewing Officer [RO]]. The
purpose of the review is to see if any grounds exist
for referring the summary finding to the SAC.

In addition, it also identifies disciplinary trends and
issues to help achieve a 'common approach' to
summary findings and punishments.

However, there is no indication – as yet - as to how
many of the reviews result in a further hearing.

Apart therefore where the accused himself refers
the findings to the SAC, or where the RO does so,
the accused will be unaware of any findings made
by the RO.

Among other things, the RO will establish that [a]

the case could be dealt with summarily, [b] the powers of punishment were not exceeded and [c] were appropriate to the rank of the accused and commensurate with the offence proved and that, where appropriate, HA was obtained.

Encouraging as this is, there is no indication that the RO is any better qualified that the CO and that, where the summary hearing record is for any reason deficient, it may not give a clear picture of the oral evidence inter alia, as one would certainly expect were court stenographers engaged – highly unlikely – and of course, the summing-up by the CO before his verdict may also give the RO some cause for concern, as indeed do those of even experienced Judges.

One issue not addressed; the CO will have had sight of the accused's 'previous' and it may have influenced his finding of guilt which of course, under normal circumstances in a civilian court, would not be the case.

Further, there is every likelihood that the CO will have some impression of the accused's character possibly even before any charge was laid, as the closed community such as one finds on any military base, does suggest that such knowledge is easy to come by either by accident or by enquiry.

The remainder of this chapter is devoted to procedural matters.

Chapters 16 to 26 cover matters not within the scope of this research[37].

Chapter 27. The Summary Appeal Court [SAC] is established to hear appeals against findings and sentence. It is generally bound by the Rules of

---

37 See footnote 3

Evidence as apply in England and Wales; it also comprises lay members but includes a Judge advocate.

There is no need to discuss this chapter further, as it does not form part of the research save as to make the point that an appeal will be heard under rules substantially different from those at the summary hearing.

Document 5.

Minor Administrative Action [JSP833]

MAA is action taken to '*rehabilitate, censure or initiate sanctions to correct professional or personal failings*'. It is a summary process, and applies the Service Test i.e., 'have the actions of a Service person adversely affected the efficiency or effectiveness of the Service'.

There is a distinction between disciplinary and administrative action in that the former is used where there has been an offence and the latter is used to set straight 'professional and personal' shortcomings.
One could suggest there is a narrow distinction between the two, and indeed common sense would suggest that is the case especially in view of the fact that there is also Major Administrative Action for cases where such action and disciplinary action are not exclusive [where as MAA and disciplinary action are]. Major administrative action would be appropriate where there are several occasions where MAA has been used against a service person.

However, this is academic, as the real point in

raising this issue is because quite minor ranks can impose MAA on lower ranks and bearing in mind the Service environment and the [sometimes] real abuse of authority, MAA does require some comment and will be addressed in the dissertation.

Note that the JSP is used as a basis for dealing with 'minor professional and *personal* [our italics] failings of performance; ergo, it should not be used as a group punishment, and this does of course apply to all proceedings whether CM, summary or MAA.

A case of MAA being administered unfairly will be dealt with in the thesis.

One positive note is that all records of MAA carried out on an individual on a training unit are destroyed on completion of training which to a degree mitigates the otherwise bad start to a recruit's service, or in other circumstances are retained for at least two years – which actually means very little.

Documents 6

Rights for accused under the Service Justice System [SJS]

This is a booklet which purports to be of assistance to the accused. However, there are several issue which require consideration and these will be covered at length in the dissertation but a few are noted here; firstly, the accused is entitled to request a copy of the MSL – a document of over 1000 pages; he is also to be given a copy of the JSP 838 – the Armed Forces Legal Aid Scheme; this is also a substantial document.

Under normal circumstances, this would not be an issue but where he can pay for legal advice, no lawyer can be present for him at the hearing, so his AAO [Accused Assisting Officer] may well be tasked with presenting the advice the accused's solicitor or barrister has prepared which would a substantial burden – finding a way round all the 'legalese' is a task in itself - in respect of his duties to the accused.

Document 7.

Support Available for Service Personnel arrested or charged with offences under the SJS.

This is a single sheet which is, in essence, a summary of the information set out in document six above, but which includes information for families [services welfare schemes], medical and spiritual etc. Apart from that it does not add anything of any value for the accused.

Documents 8 and 9

Magistrates' Courts Procedure and The Magistrates' Courts Rules

The initial training of Magistrates and the guidance throughout their careers is overseen by the Judicial College. The process is constantly 'hands-on' and is far removed from the training of the COs tasked with the administration of summary justice on his unit or detachment.

This point is at the very centre of this research; the question which arises here is, and bearing in mind the far-reaching effect on a serviceman convicted under the COs regime, does the CO and his staff have between them the ability, knowledge and are they able to be impartial enough to deal fairly with an accuses who is not entitled to legal representation and who may well feel intimidated by the situation in which he finds himself ?

It appears *prima facia* that the Service training – a two-week course at most - is grossly inadequate especially bearing in mind that the CO has many other responsibilities to discharge in his working day.

Regarding the documents which relate to the Magistrates' courts and training, it is of interest here as this sets out, albeit briefly, the standard of the summary justice, the personnel involved, and has to be taken as the benchmark of summary justice delivery. It offers several contrasts when read against the SJS within HM forces.

Training is over a period of 12 to 18 months which will include visits to prisons and observations in active courts and there is almost constant mentoring. There are appraisals every three years, and continuation training on new legislation.

Magistrates[38] training is based on competences and is on-going throughout a Magistrates career. The Courts Committee provides the governance and oversight for the training of Magistrates to ensure that there is consistency at local, regional and national level. The committee also oversees the training of District Judges, court clerks and 'legal advisors'. Their Criminal Sub-committee identifies the needs of adult criminal and youth courts.

---

38 Courts and Tribunals Judiciary

The Magistrates' Courts Procedure [Magistrates' Courts Rules 1981] sets out in detail the conduct of summary trial and bearing in mind that the substantial authority vested in Magistrates, and in COs, where in each case the decisions as to conviction and sentencing can have a considerable effect on a person's life / career then as a civilian, the disparity in training is remarkable

In a number of ways, however, the courts procedure mirrors that of the SJS in that the Magistrates deal with summary [minor] offences where there is no right generally for the accused to elect trial by a higher court [the Crown Court in civilian cases and CM in the Service], either-way offences dealt with by Magistrates or crown court / summary CO's hearing or CM, and those 'indictable' offences which are crown court / CM only.

What this research has to do is to set out how – if at all – the differences lead to inequity for the Serviceman and also to highlight any other 'anomalies' which either do, or appear to, disfavour the military offender.

Conclusion.

The research question centres on the proposal that the summary justice as applied to Service personnel[39] is does not comprise a fair system. The reason for this assumption is that the process is in many respects far removed from the 'accepted' norm as seen as practised in England and Wales via the Magistrates' courts.

---

39 Which included civilians subject to service discipline

Each of the issues which confirm this view will be thoroughly aired in the dissertation.
Briefly that will include the following;

The process is inquisitorial.

The accused Commanding Officer, in whom is vested the power to hear charges summarily, undergoes a short course in the basics of the law, believed to be in the region of 10 working days. As regard this, precise details will be set out as soon as the MOD furnish the material.

The AAO - also a layman, as lawyers are prohibited from taking on that role - are expected to take on quite a burden for the accused, who may not anyway be in a position to pay for the services of a solicitor.

The accused is not entitled to any legal representation during the hearings.

The process can be daunting for a junior rank finding himself in front of his CO; this could be an aircraftsman, probably still a teenager, and the lowest rank in the Royal Air Force, in front of a wing commander [or other Service's equivalents] and such a 'confrontation' will almost certainly mean the accused will not be best able to give a good account of himself.

Under such circumstances, proper, legal representation is essential to account for this, a role no AAO can fulfil as he, too, may also feel intimidated to a degree.

The CO will have a record of the accused's disciplinary record; such information is not given to the courts until after a finding.

The CO can, once the matter has been referred to HA, pass a sentence of up to 90 days detention; in civilian terms this equates to a six-month term of imprisonment, the maximum a Magistrate can hand down.

In addition, the case can be such that the PNC can be passed details of the offence and sentence, so seriously prejudicing the offender's career as a civilian after leaving the forces.

Unless a MMA [Minor Administrative Action] which should remain on the accused's record / file for at least two years, or where the MMA was taken at a training unit [when it is removed on posting] the record of punishment stays with the accused's record throughout his service career. This will understandably, seriously prejudice his chances of promotion.

A Service unit is a very closed society, and a person accused of an offence, criminal or disciplinary, could well feel uncomfortable under the circumstances which prevail; for example, he could still be attending training or operational duties but still subject to detention pending any hearing.

At least as a civilian, he would be away from any overly oppressive social environment; few people will recognise him as an offender [if e.g., on bail].

Finally, and in view of the rather poor recruitment rate for HM Forces, the Services cannot afford to be seen to perpetrate a system of summary justice which is, or seems to be, inherently unfair, as this will encourage recruits to apply to leave the service or not 'give of their best' under operational circumstances.

Family members may be involved in the taking of such a serious move, and might in most cases feel that their child should leave the Forces if they too, feel his treatment was unfair. They may regard it as a form of bullying.

After research, the above may give rise to a number of recommendations which will if accepted, result in a more evenly balanced, hence fair, process for the application of summary justice.

BIBLIOGRAPHY

Armed Forces Bill Team [MOD] An overview of the Service Justice System [SJS] and the Armed Forces Act.

Armed Forces Act [the Act] 2006 Chapter 52 TSO

Explanatory Notes AFA 2006 TSO

Manual of Service Law [MSL] [JSP 830] Volume 1 Chapters 1 to 15 and Chapter 27

Minor Administrative Action [JSP 833] MOD October 2008 [Nov 2014]

Rights for accused under the Service Justice System [SJS] [Booklet]

Support Available for Service Personnel arrested or charged with offences under the SJS

The Armed Forces Legal Aid Scheme JSP 838 Pt 1 – Directive [December 2014] Armed Forces Criminal Legal Aid Authority

The Armed Forces Legal Aid Scheme JSP 838 Pt 2
– Guidance [December 2014] Armed Forces
Criminal Legal Aid Authority

Magistrates' Courts Procedure 1981
Magistrates' Courts Rules, The 1981
Mwedzi, P; UCLAN student Master of Laws,
November 2014 in his article 'Demystifying the
British Military Justice System'

Findlay [v The United Kingdom [1997]]

<u>Research Proposal and Ethical Guidelines</u>

<u>Research Title</u>

'The Summary Justice process as applied in H.M. Armed Forces does not offer the same safeguards available to defendants in civilian courts and is therefore inherently unfair to the accused'.

<u>Summary</u>

This research will examine the summary justice system [SJS] from the perspective of its being sufficiently removed from the court practices and procedures applied in the civilian courts, and which operate to ensure that nobody is convicted of any offence where there is any doubt as to his guilt. This is not a simple concept; a determination of guilt or innocence by applying the law is alien to a layman, so cannot be applied where, as with service summary justice, no party is required to have legal qualifications.

Summary justice is applied in the Forces, whether before an accused's Commanding Officer or at the Minor Administrative Action [MAA] level e.g., personal failings, or via minor disciplinary hearings. All applications must be fair on the accused and with a right to have such cases reviewed by a higher authority.

This research will show where the procedures fail to meet the fairness test and will demonstrate how the processes can be revised to operate within the existing structures but with more supervision over the review process and at the same time reducing the need for offenders to appeal their cases to go through the protracted process of a full Summary Appeal Court [SAC] hearing.

The literature for this research is the Manual of Service Law [MSL] and the Armed Forces Act 2006 [The Act], and the Magistrates' Courts Rules. Input come from various authorities, namely the Judge Advocate General's office [JAGO], the Service Prosecution Authority [SPA], the Military Court Service [MCS], the Director of Legal Services [DLS] and RAF College Cranwell.

Research Aims

To examine the hypothesis that the SJS is unfair on the accused. If proved, or sufficiently so, to show unfairness, it will be incumbent upon the several authorities whose joint task is to oversee the SJS to seriously consider the paper and take on board the proposals for reform or at least address the most important features. If this is the outcome, then this research will be a successful and worthwhile project.

Currently, the criticism levelled at the SJS by various bodies is motive enough to pursue these points, and with the legislation emanating from Europe, in particular the European Ct. of Humans Rights [ECtHR], it cannot be long before change will Force the government to undertake wide-reaching reform, which should be commenced sooner rather than have the MOD et al face the embarrassment of being forced to do so later. A case in point is Findlay-v-UK [1997] which brought about serious reform in the Courts Martial [CM] procedures but it will be shown that issues which brought about those changes are still manifest in the SJ process.

An immediate move would be to ensure that all personnel involved are suitably qualified or, in the alternative, revise the other procedures currently in Force and which do not profess to be any kind of judicial process, viz., the Minor Administrative Actions and the Major Administrative Actions [to include the former Army General Administrative Instruction 67 - AGAI67] to deal with all summary offences. All serious issues would be reserved for Courts Martial where qualified professionals run the courts along lines more familiar to the civilian practitioners.

Research Proposal

Introduction

The civilian criminal justice system in the UK is operated by law professionals, who apply the law and who overseen by a higher authority to ensure the law is applied correctly. It is an adversarial system, whereby the prosecution and the defence set out their cases and can challenge each other's submissions.

The Service JS does not mirror that of the Magistrates' courts; those persons who hear the cases are not law practitioners. Their authority derives from The Act. Notwithstanding, the consequences of a summary conviction can be as serious for an offender as any civilian conviction in that criminal offence and some non-criminal offences will be recorded on the police national computer.

Discipline has always been tough in the military and

in many cases rightly so, as there is within any military unit an understanding that a command must and will be obeyed if the unit is to have the ability to operate as a cohesive force.

Consider the Army Leadership Code - An Introductory Guide describes discipline as ...

> *"The maintenance of operational effectiveness"* and
> *"The primary antidote to fear... it is supported by team loyalty, trust and professionalism. Discipline instils self-confidence and self-control. Good discipline means soldiers will do the right thing even under the most difficult of circumstances; "To maintain our legitimacy, all ranks are required to operate within the law. UK criminal law applies wherever soldiers are serving, and military law has embraced all civil offences.* [In this context 'civil' means the criminal law as dispensed by the civilian courts. Civil can mean non-criminal jurisdiction such as is used for employment law and torts and contract law inter alia] *When deployed on operations, soldiers are subject to international law, including the laws of armed conflict, the prescribed rules of engagement and in some cases local, civil law. Taken together, such laws establish the baseline for the standards of personal conduct of the soldier as a citizen".*

But the serviceman even now is not getting a fair hearing on disciplinary and criminal matters when heard by a Service summary court. Why this state of affairs exists is hard to determine, but there are indications of a degree of dissatisfaction with the status quo.

With a rise in litigation fuelled by Legal Aid, with campaigning newspapers, the ECtHR, the Universal Declaration of Human Rights [UDHR], nobody, whatever his standing, and however lowly, has to tolerate ill-treatment whatever his circumstances, and nobody whoever he is, can inflict, in any sense, unfair treatment on anybody.

This must apply to the serviceman working under extreme conditions in many different environments, often in war zones, but still with a need to be disciplined effectively, at home or overseas. Wherever disciplinary matters are dealt by a Commanding Officer in the cool surroundings of an office, the serviceman still has a right to be treated fairly.

The research will be gathering evidence to provide sufficient reason to get the Service to recognise the drawbacks in the Summary system and why the procedures should be revised even though, more than a decade ago, and, more recently, they have been severely criticised, but notwithstanding, there have been no meaningful changes to the summary process..

The System

1. The first point about the SJS is that the Commanding Officer [CO] sits as Judge and jury, most certainly a breach of Article 6 of the European Convention of Human Rights [ECHR]. He will not have had any meaningful education in the law and nor will the Accused's Assisting Officer [AAO]. No lawyers feature at the summary hearing.
Prior to any hearing the accused can apply for assistance from one of the many law firms which undertake military case-work, but the accused is

not permitted at summary hearings to be represented by a lawyer, but is allowed his AAO and access to the Manual of Service Law [MSL] and to the Act, and to a DVD which sets out, in a very simplified form, what the accused can expect at the hearing of his case.

2. In 2012 a report [by a serving Army officer] was undertaken for the Defence Select Committee [DSC] for its investigation into how the service handles complaints and discipline. Members of Parliament who comprise the DSC were expected to produce their findings a year after the report. However, the only 2013 report as far as legal issues are concerned, is the 'UK Armed Forces Personnel and the Legal Framework for Future Operations' 'and it concentrated on the Iraq Historical Allegations Team [IHAT] and procedures regarding the prosecution of the alleged offenders. As no relevant report has been unearthed, it is more than likely that the 2012 report was a British Armed Forces Federation [BAFF] paper sent to the DSC on the 25th February 2013.

The report was was picked up by Kris Jepson and aired on Channel 4 news. The author, his rank and his job in the Army unknown, averred that Army discipline was rarely transparent or accountable, was frequently unlawful in the way it handled complaints and discipline and called for an overhaul of an Army procedure [then] known as Army General Administrative Instruction 67 [AGAI 67] now superseded by Minor Administrative Action [MAA or Major Administrative Action], but essentially the same procedure.

Of the same report, Rojas [Daily Telegraph, 22 November 2012] commented "The service [Army *and the AGAI67 system - part of the SJ process*] was 'frequently unlawful' in its handling of complaints and internal sanctions proceedings" and the Ministry of Defence had ignored the lessons of Deepcut, the Surrey barracks where four recruits died amid claims of a culture of bullying.

The Jepson report made the following charges; no safeguards to protect junior personnel from the chain of command; nothing to prevent dishonest commanders from pursuing vendettas against those working under them; service lawyers questioned the legality of using the system; it breached Article 6 of the ECHR. Equivalent civilian disciplinary systems are governed by ACAS rules. It concluded that the AGAI 67 should be rewritten [it became the MAA commonly used by the services]. So much for the handling of minor administrative matters.

To reinforce this ECHR issue, Gerry Rubin in *'Why Military law ? Some UK Perspectives'* cites the case of Martin v UK [2002 34 EHRR 1253], where a British civilian dependant, his father a serviceman based in in Germany, was tried in the CM and was convicted of murder. He appealed. The conviction was held to be a violation of article 6 of the ECHR [see 1 above] on the grounds that the composition, structure and procedure of the court martial were sufficient to raise serious concern as to the court's lack of independence and its impartiality.

An earlier case, that of Findlay [App 22107/93 [1997] 24 EHRR 22], brought about a substantial change, and even before the final hearing, at which Findlay succeeded, the then JAG [James Rant] knew he was on the back-foot and worked on new legislation which became the Armed

Forces Act 2006 [effective October 2009] although this did little to deal with the summary process.

The MAA, a summary process one step below the CO hearing level, as operated is fine in theory, but empirical evidence shows that it does come close to the description of the AGAI67 in that it is easy for even junior NCOs to use it for other than wholly legitimate purposes and that the Officer reviewer can be too close to the complainant in his review of the outcome. This is clearly wrong and, where obvious, it does raise the hackles of the 'offender' and is more likely to make him seriously question his future in the Forces, and, as will be shown, training establishments can be particular prone to this 'illicit' use of the MAA procedure.

The same charges which were made by the ECHR in the Martin appeal can also be levelled at summary proceedings, bearing in mind inter alia the very 'closed' society in which the hearings are conducted. In addition, if the same Article 6 argument were to be made at a Summary Appeal Court [SAC] hearing, any defence lawyer would certainly raise the *Martin v UK* case in his submissions.

3. The summary court can hear criminal as well as disciplinary cases. However, and bearing in mind the constitution of the hearing, a conviction by this summary process can mean the offence being recorded on the Police National Computer [PNC]. On this PNC point, Louise Brooke-Holland in *'The Military Justice System: an introduction'* [Standard Note SN06823 House of Commons Library 2012 [International Affairs and Defence section]] stated [at 1.9 - Police records] that …

'...Some people were unaware that their Summary or CM convictions were recorded on the PNC until they had left the Service and encountered problems with visa or job applications ...'.

Of even more concern, is that some non-criminal offences can be recorded on the PNC [MSL Chapter 9 para.115 Recording of offences on the PNC]. A full list of offences recordable is at Annex Q to this same chapter.

This is clearly unsatisfactory, and one could surmise that if an accused had been made aware of that fact, he might well have chosen to either appeal his summary conviction or have elected for trail by CM in the first place and bearing in mind that the summary hearings conviction rate is 95% [JAG's office May 2017] with CM conviction rate 50% it would appear to be the better option for the accused.

A Colonel at a meeting at the Joint Services Command and Staff College [JSCSC] is reported as saying, *"If soldiers knew about the difference in conviction rate, they would never elect for summary hearing"* and if they were to *"It would 'break' the courts martial system".*

The JAG's office commented only that *'... it would come under some strain ...'.* The Service Prosecution Authority web site deals with this issue by saying ...

'No prosecution authority can predict the level of crime or the volume of cases which will be referred to it in a given year. In the case of the

SPA there are clearly risks in terms of case-flow. It is conceivable that the changes made by the Act [Armed Forces Act 2006] may see a reduction in summary dealing, and a higher volume of cases being referred to the SPA. Where COs follow proper procedure, are alert to their responsibilities, and are able to instil trust in those under command, summary dealing, or minor administrative action can still be both an effective and appropriate manner of dealing with less serious criminal or disciplinary offences. Reducing delay is a key aim of the Service Justice System. It remains the intention that Service law should reflect the provisions of the civilian justice system as far as it is sensible and practical to do so. This involves recognition of the need to sustain Service ethos and discipline. Attention to detail in preserving the best and changing those procedures which do not serve us well, will be another target of our attention in the years ahead.'

Those facing a summary hearing are, if the AAO is doing his job, advised of their rights to opt for court martial, but the report claims that the circumstances of the accused *vis-à-vis* the command chain, and with the assistance of an unqualified AAO who may himself be under some pressure to have the case dealt with, and the need felt by the accused *et al* to get the matter over with, means any subtle, if not direct, pressure to do so does not offer a genuinely free choice. The MOD counter this allegation with the defence that soldiers *'... make informed decisions to opt for summary hearings ...'.*

This sound fine, but the need to get the business

over within days, is a motivation rather than having a delay of perhaps several weeks, being the time it may take to convene a court martial. The JAG's office accepts that it takes 'too long to bring to hearing'.

4.   The summary process is inquisitorial not adversarial. In countries where the former operates, it is always handled by a *Judge* who decides the scope and range of a hearing, searches for facts, listens to witnesses examines documents, orders evidence to be taken and then makes such further inquiries as he deems necessary. A layman can hardly exercise the same degree of expertise necessary to arrive at a reliable conclusion, viz., the same as may be reached by an experienced, legal practitioner.

The adversarial process, as practised in the UK, is one where each party has responsibility for finding and presenting their evidence. The Judge / Magistrate does not investigate the facts. The summary procedure as used in HM Forces falls between two stools; at chapter 11 MSL it states that ' *...the summary hearing is not a court and the rules of evidence do not apply ...'* but does this absolve them from having to involve themselves in the detailed procedures which are exercised in the civil courts and which are to ensure there is no miscarriage of justice, that the dealings with an accused are fair ?

Even a modest law dictionary gives 52 definitions of evidence, starting with 'evidence' and finishing with 'evidence unsworn' and 'evidential facts'; every text on the English Legal system is peppered with references to evidence. A casual observer might not be overly concerned about this treatment of evidence by the SJS but every lawyer will take a different view especially where, and as mooted supra, the summary conviction can have the same consequences for the offender as a civil court conviction; why the two widely differing procedures?

Lawyer or layman, a hypothetical, ordinary and reasonable person, 'the man on the Clapham omnibus' the fair and reasonable man who represents no more than the anthropomorphic conception of justice - might regard such a position as unfair.

Added to this, the officers who are destined for posts as Commanding Officers have a basic introduction to the MSL and the Act, beyond that he receives during basic training, but this cannot even approach endowing them with adequate knowledge to sit in Judgement on his men and to arrive at a fair, reasoned conclusion as to guilt or otherwise. It is no good him applying 'common sense'; it is no good him being intelligent; he has to apply a degree of knowledge about the law, the circumstances of the offence amongst many other considerations. An impossible task which commits him to operating under the dark cloud of ignorance of the law.

On this, Rant [1.09;] …

> *'The time when the criminal law could be easily assimilated and applied with a dash of common sense by unqualified people even if of outstanding intelligence, has long since passed'...*

The CO might be of outstanding intelligence, and have had a little training, but he can pass down to a junior officer the authority to hear summary cases, and the likelihood of that junior officer being equally intelligent and with same understanding of legal principles, of guilt or innocence or for him to remain utterly impartial and to find on the strength of evidence [as perceived by him] is unlikely and, if an ex-Cranwell cadet, his introduction to Service law comes a poor second to his flying or engineering training.

Nor is is any good the CO and his team applying the maxim so often propounded by the Rt. Honourable Lord Denning, [MR,1962 to 1982] that he 'was interested in justice, not the law'. The great Judge came from a totally different perspective, and it was not from one of ignorance.

5.   We are equal in the eyes of the law but not, apparently, in the eyes of the Service law. Article 7 of the Universal Declaration of Human Rights [UDHR] states …

> *'We are all equal before the law and are entitled without any discrimination to equal protection of the law. Thus, everyone must be treated equally regardless of race, gender, national origin, colour, ethnicity, religion, disability or other characteristics without privilege, discrimination or bias'...*

To which one can add *rank*.

The MSL at chapter 13 Annex B lists 'Punishments which may be awarded to each rank or rate' and lists the ranks from Officer, Warrant Officer, Senior non-commissioned officers, corporals, leading / lance corporals and able rates / marines / soldiers and airmen with the punishments covering forfeiture of seniority [Officers only] then fines, severe reprimand, reprimand, admonition, Service compensation order, Reduction in rank [not officers] Stoppage of leave, detention, payment orders [Able rates etc. only !] and restriction of privileges [Able etc rates only!].

There may be some rationale behind this, but it appears to fly in the face of the equality principle.

6. The Armed Forces are made up of very wide social and intellectual classes. Some officers and other ranks join with degrees; other applicants need only to show an education level 2, which is approximately that of an 8 to 11 year old.
Some can join at age 16, perhaps immature, viz., *lacking wisdom insight or stability because of youth, being the period between childhood and maturity.* There is then, with the newer, and younger recruits, the question of their vulnerability.

Being in a Service environment can affect different people in different ways. Unfortunately, any person who is seen to be vulnerable is a prime target for all sorts of unhealthy, mischievous pranksters, to the point that the victim could be driven to all sorts behaviour which will very possibly lead to him standing in front of his CO. Will the CO appreciate this ? Will he know how to deal with the case beyond the guidelines set down in chapter 12 MSL 'Defences, mitigation and criminal responsibility'?

It is not an easy call, and, as suggested above, there will be a burden on the CO to come to a decision based not on the facts and surrounding circumstances, but one which sees him [possibly] siding with his NCOs - in disciplinary cases - or the

Service Police in criminal cases.

7.   There is no mention in the MSL of rehabilitation of offenders. The 1974 Rehabilitation of Offenders' Act gives certain directions regarding when an offence is spent, and, with the exception of certain occupations, there comes a time when past offences do not have to be disclosed to e.g., a prospective employer.

Apart from that, the Act gives the offender a 'second chance' and where a serviceman is looking forward to a full career in the military, one should suppose that he would have the same or better right as regards 'past misdemeanour's, but this is not the case. Promotion, commissioning from the ranks, all require a clean sheet, or at least no serious offences, to be shown but the printed record of every serviceman is available even long after the person's retirement from the Force or even after his death.

In addition, and as mooted above, some offences both criminal and non-criminal, can be recorded on the PNC. It can certainly be the case that the soldier, sailor or airman might consider there is no future in his remaining in the Force, and so leave at the first opportunity. This is of special significance today when there is a serious shortfall in recruiting, so it seems that, where past offences are a factor in a decision to leave, consideration should be given to 'levelling the playing field'.

Some light on this unsatisfactory situation is shed by the JAG's office - 'the situation is under review'.

The Way Forward

To deal with the perceived anomalies in the

SJS, and depending on the outcome of the research, it may be necessary that some or all of the following are addressed;

[a] That the CO's current role in taking summary hearings in criminal cases and on not guilty please be abolished;
[b] That the MAA and Major Admin Actions [but with Major Admin Actions, i.e., not just being personal failings, having a right to CM trial] be upgraded to deal with the current summary cases but not as any kind of judicial proceedings, and with serious cases going straight to CM;
[c] That Officers' review of MAA cases be properly administered and overseen by senior Officers;
[d] No service convictions recorded on the PNC;
[e] That a form of the Rehabilitation of Offenders' Act 1974 be introduced and irrelevant or spent offences are shown on the serviceman's record so not not available to the CO's summary hearing.
[f] That the Service Complaints Commissioner [Ombudsman] be authorised to deal with issues emanating from any MAA and Major Admin. Actions;
[g] Servicemen under the age of 18 or if otherwise regarded as 'vulnerable' should have a second assistant who is there solely to look after the welfare of the accused.

On completion of the research, and in writing-up the dissertation, other main issues could be added to this list or some removed.

Ethics

This research is mostly a literary study, and is based substantially on, the MSL and the Act, the Statutory Instrument 1981 No. 552 - Magistrates'

Court Procedure / Magistrates' Courts Rules and with numerous other documents available from Her Majesty's Stationary Office [TSO] or via other publishers. In addition, information gained at interview will be deemed to come from the authority concerned and not the individual respondent and any publication of that material will be attributed to that authority unless the researcher is notified otherwise, and this point will be made at the relevant time. Any necessary departure from this will be notified to the Ethics Committee of the Faculty of Humanities and Social Sciences but, apart from that possible event, it is not considered that any application to the Committee is required with the methods currently employed or to be employed in the future.

Regarding direct input from authorities such as the Judge Advocate General's office, the Service Prosecution Authority, the Military Court Service, the Director of Legal Services and RAF College Cranwell, they all represent different aspects of the SJS or the justice system as a whole, so no one questionnaire will not be applicable to all of them. Any questions posed will be relevant to their roles, and any overlap will be cross-referred. They will be given the opportunity to review their answers, but their responses will not be attributed to any individual.

Interviews with servicemen who have been put through the summary justice process would not be appropriate, as it is mainly with the system itself that this research is concerned, not the personnel who have experienced it but some interesting comments have been recorded but these will not be attributed in the dissertation, but made available for authentication purposes if called for.

Technical / Resource Issues.

The Service Prosecution Authority, the Military Court Service and the Director of Legal Services have recently positively responded to approaches. An interview has been conducted with the Judge Advocate General and his input attached as an annex to the dissertation. There was a meeting with the Director, Military Court Service [MCS]; response has been received from the SPA and from the Director Legal Services.

Bibliography

Brooke-Holland, L *'The Military Justice System: an introduction'* House of Commons [International Affairs and Defence section] 2012

Denning, Baron, A.T; January 1899 – March 1999

Featherstone, D, *'All for a Shilling a Day'* [1966, Jarrolds]

Jepson, K; Channel 4 news reporter.

Martin; *Martin v UK [ECHR App no. 40426/98 October 2006]*

Pigot, Captain, HM *'Hermione' 1797.*

Rant , J; The Court martial and Service Law [3rd Ed] HHJ Blackett 2009

Rodger, N.A.M.[Exeter University] *'The Command of the Ocean'* Penguin Books 2004.

Rojas [Daily Telegraph, 22 November 2012] 'The service *[Army and the AGAI67 system]*'

Rubin, G; *'Why Military law ? Some UK Perspectives'*